NORTH AMERICAN BIRD WATCHING FOR BEGINNERS

NORTH AMERICAN BIRD WATCHING
for beginners

Field Notes on 150 Species to
Start Your Birding Adventures

Sharon Stiteler

ROCKRIDGE
PRESS

For general information on our other products and services or to obtain technical support, please contact our Customer Care Department within the United States at (866) 744-2665, or outside the United States at (510) 253-0500.

Rockridge Press publishes its books in a variety of electronic and print formats. Some content that appears in print may not be available in electronic books, and vice versa.

Interior and Cover Designer: Jami Spittler
Art Producer: Sue Bischofberger
Editor: Anne Goldberg
Production Editor: Caroline Flanagan
Production Manager: Riley Hoffman

Photography used under license from shutterstock.com and iStockphoto.com, except Chimney Swift, p. 71, © AGAMI Photo Agency / Alamy Stock Photo. Illustrations used under license from shutterstock.com.

Paperback ISBN: 978-1-63878-348-0
    eBook ISBN: 978-1-63878-903-1
R0

FOR CURT RAWN.

Birds and Beers wouldn't be what it is without you, my very dear friend.

CONTENTS

FOUR

FIVE

SIX

Introduction

BIRDS ARE MY FIRST AND TRUE LOVE.
It started with an illustration of a pileated woodpecker in a field guide when I was seven. I knew woodpeckers were a type of bird, but it blew my mind that one could be as big as a crow. I would spend hours going over the illustrations, imagining what it must be like to see one in real life. I would quiz myself on the silhouettes shown in the front and the back of the book. Little did I know that those quizzes prepped me for the day I saw a meadowlark perched on a wire and freaked my parents out as I screamed, "MEADOWLARK!" from the back seat of the car. I had no idea the sheer variety of birds a person could see in the United States. Birds can be giant like a condor, tiny like a hummingbird, colorful like a painted bunting, or downright weird like an ibis.

Their beauty can be measured not only in appearance but also in sound. The haunting song of a wood thrush is seared into the summer memories of people who aren't even birders. When I would see a new bird or witness a behavior described in a book, it was like seeing a celebrity. I marveled that a killdeer would pretend to have a broken wing exactly like the books had told me.

One gray day in winter in Indianapolis, my mother called me from the kitchen in a very excited voice: "Sharon! Quick, come down. What is this?!" It was a northern flicker, a bird I had observed many times but which was entirely new to my mother. She knew what a woodpecker was, but seeing one so large with its black spots, red patch on the back of the head, and flashy yellow wings really struck her. She bragged to everyone about this new bird. And that's when my mom's birding journey began. She prefers what she sees in the yard, whereas I wander the world to find them.

Birding can be done anywhere and at any time of year, at any age, even in the busiest cities. I saw my very first crissal thrasher a half hour after stepping off a plane in Las Vegas. I've spied American woodcocks in Central Park in Manhattan. Birding will put you in tune with nature in a new way. You will get a heightened sense of the shift of seasons as you note when birds arrive and leave, when they nest, and what seeds and insects are available when certain birds raise young. You will be engaging in an activity that constantly teaches you something new about nature, occasionally frustrates you with its taxonomy rules and changes, and always wows you with its beauty.

This is an introductory book to whet your appetite for birding. If I gave you all the information to identify all the birds, this book would weigh 15 pounds and be terrifying. This book starts with the very basic yet amazing facts. I'm excited to introduce you to a world that has captivated and been a source of comfort to me for almost my entire life. Birds treat everyone the same, and all are welcome. This is a lifelong endeavor if you want it to be. You can enjoy birds in your own way, from taking joy in the behaviors of crows in the backyard to trying to chase every rare bird in your state. It's a passion that can take you in so many directions but will always thrill you.

ONE GETTING TO KNOW OUR FEATHERED FRIENDS

Before you begin birding, it will help you to understand a few basics about birds. This chapter will give you that foundation. It covers how birds' bodies work and how they function in their environments. It also delves into the basics of feeding, nesting, range, migration, and grooming.

THE WORD ON BIRDS

Birds come in all shapes and sizes, from the mothlike humming-bird to the giant, gangly heron. Each one is unique in its lifestyle, behavior, song, and color; birding is so rewarding because there's always something new to explore and learn. It's impossible to do it all at once, but if you start small—focus on three new facts a week, or a goal like sighting three types of warblers each spring—you'll gain a lot of insight and have a lifelong adventure of birding fun.

Identifying birds is not just about color. Two of the most important aspects of identifying a bird are the location it was observed and the time of year it was seen. Some birds are only in certain areas of North America at certain times of year. Take this example: Loggerhead shrikes and northern shrikes look almost identical. If you are seeing a shrike in Wisconsin in January, it's going to be a northern shrike. If you are seeing one in July, it's likely a loggerhead.

Along with location, behavior can also separate similar species. House finches and purple finches look identical to birders just learning the ropes. If you live in Indiana and see a brown streaky finch with pinkish red on its head and chest and it has made a nest in your hanging plant basket, that is a house finch and not a purple finch. Purple finches nest farther north and usually in a conifer.

But let's back up and start with some fundamentals about bird anatomy, bird behavior, and birding vocabulary. That way, you'll be able to start seeing—and talking—like a birder.

Birding Life: Some History

Bird taxonomy (classification) is still developing in scientific circles, but the most recent research suggests that birds evolved from dinosaurs in the Jurassic period, specifically theropods. That's right; that robin you see hopping around your lawn evolved from the same common ancestor as a *Tyrannosaurus rex*.

Bird taxonomy is changing all the time as new species are discovered or as DNA research reveals that two separate species are actually the same species. There are roughly 10,000 species of birds in the world, and over 900 species of birds can be found in North America. This book focuses on the most common birds you are likely to encounter, divided into the following:

COMMON BIRDS: Birds you could easily spot in your backyard

SONGBIRDS (PARK BIRDS): Birds you may have to travel to a local park to find

WATERBIRDS: Birds associated with bodies of water

RAPTORS: Birds of prey that generally have large talons and hooked beaks

Birding itself didn't begin until the invention of opera glasses in the early 1800s. Before that, the only way to see birds closely was when they were killed. Today, we get to see them in action, as they were meant to be.

BIRD BASICS

Even within a given species, there can be a lot of variation in the way birds look. But there are some rules that commonly apply when considering the differences between males and females and between adults and juveniles.

Adults and Juveniles

Generally, young birds are less colorful than the adults. This characteristic makes them less of a target to predators and serves as a sign to other birds that they are not good mating material. In birds of prey, the tail feathers and wing feathers of juveniles can be longer than those of adult birds. One evolutionary explanation for this difference is that young birds are going to crash-land a lot, and those protective feathers will see a lot of wear and tear until the next molt (growth of new feathers).

When young birds leave the nest, they are as big as they are going to get, usually the same weight as the adults, if not a little larger. Some birds leave the nest a few days before they can fly and have shorter wings and tails, but they grow out in about a week. You might even see a little remaining down at this stage. Some birds reach maturity faster than others. Cardinals molt into adult plumage before their first winter, whereas a bald eagle takes five years to molt into the white head and tail.

Males and Females

There is some commonality between species in differences between male and female birds. For instance, in most species, females are less colorful than males. They do a majority of the incubation, so because they sit in one spot several hours a day, many days in a row, it helps to blend in. There are exceptions, like the Wilson's phalarope, but in that case, the male incubates the eggs.

In terms of size, it varies. In swans, usually the female is smaller in the pair. But in birds of prey, the female is larger than the male. With some species, such as Cooper's hawks and peregrine falcons, the female can be a third larger than the male. In other words, size is not really indicative of sex in birds, because it varies between individual birds.

A unique and interesting example is the white-throated sparrow, which has two color "morphs": bold black and white on top, or dull tan and buff. The brighter birds tend to be more aggressive and defend territory more. Duller birds of either sex tend to do more incubation and feeding. Either sex can be seen with either markings, but bright birds of either sex that pair up with duller birds have the most successful breeding season as opposed to pairs of the same color morph.

Birding Life: Bird Facts

Birds are truly amazing, especially when you realize what they are capable of doing with their bodies.

- **Some songbirds, like the wood thrush, can produce multiple songs simultaneously and harmonize with themselves.**

- **A shorebird called the bar-tailed godwit was tracked flying nonstop for eight days and 12 hours during fall migration.**

- **Studies have illustrated that both crows and pigeons can recognize individual human faces.**

- **Some birds, including pelicans, vultures, cormorants, and herons, will projectile vomit when they feel threatened.**

- **During their late summer molt, many cardinals will lose all their head feathers at once, exposing their black skin.**

HOME SWEET HABITAT

Habitat is a specific type of environment in which a bird can live. Habitat has a major influence on bird behavior and can be a starting point for identification. For instance, sanderlings run like crazy with waves when foraging on a beach but are quite calm when foraging in a freshwater marsh. Habitat can also help make sense of why birds have specific shapes. For example, birds with webbed feet like ducks will do better moving around in and on water than a cardinal or a blue jay with unwebbed toes.

Birds tend to pick a type of habitat and stick to it, but some birds will use more than one habitat. Red-winged blackbirds nest in marshes but can be found anywhere during migration. There are many types of habitats out there, but for the sake of easing you into birding, this book will focus on five types and will receive symbols that accord with their habitats:

 Woodland: Areas with lots of trees

Grassland: Open areas with few or no trees

 Scrub: Areas with lots of shrubs and grasses but no tall trees, including urban areas

Aquatic: Any water, including coasts, lakes, rivers, and ponds

Some birds favor wooded edges, so they might be categorized as both woodland and grassland. Some birds have adapted to eat mostly fish—like herons and kingfishers—and they will be listed as aquatic, even though they don't swim in the water.

RANGE

Ranges are areas on the map where a population of birds (and their habitats) can be found. Range can be determined by many factors, including geographic barriers, such as mountains, or types of habitats, such as prairies or forests. Some birds like mallards or house sparrows are generalists, meaning they can nest just about anywhere and eat foods in a variety of habitats. Other birds have a very limited diet and specific nesting requirements and can only live in very specific places, as is the case for the snail kite in southern Florida. Birds with a narrow range will be more difficult to spot. And to confuse matters a bit more, ranges can change and are shaped by migration and seasonal patterns.

Just a note on flying out of range. It is rare. It is possible for birds to fly out of range, but 99.9 percent of the time when you see a bird you can't identify and you suspect that it is a rare bird out of range, it is not. For this reason, the location you're in when trying to identify a bird is of primary importance.

MIGRATION PATTERNS

Migration is a key part of bird life and can be a factor in identification. Both spring and fall migration last many months, so it could be argued that migration never truly ends. Migration can entail moving from one continent to another, like traveling from South America to North America to raise young and then heading back home. Migration can also include going to higher elevations to nest and then returning to lower elevations in winter.

Spring migration can go from February through early June, and fall migration starts in late July and, depending on how lakes and rivers freeze up, lasts into early December. Different species of birds move at different times.

The biggest factor that influences migration is photoperiod, or the length of daylight. As days lengthen in spring, hormones are triggered in birds to move north and sing. After they arrive at their desired territory and raise young, the summer solstice happens and the days begin to grow shorter, which triggers their breeding hormones to calm down and then head south. Photoperiod also influences food availability. With longer days and warmer temperatures, berries, seeds, and insects become active and available. Many of the birds that come north for the summer are taking advantage of the abundance of insects to feed their young.

Some species, such as cranes and swans, learn their migratory routes and stopover sites from the adults, and others, including buntings and warblers, are hardwired to travel in certain directions when heading to wintering grounds. And then some birds do not migrate at all. Cardinals and chickadees, for example, do not migrate and instead spend the year in the same general area.

North American Flyways

Flyways are migratory routes. There are four major flyways in the United States: the Pacific Flyway, the Central Flyway, the Mississippi Flyway, and the Atlantic Flyway. The routes divide North America into four trails with broad ranges that birds tend to follow. Migration spans over four to five months. April and May are the busiest months for spring migration, and September and October have the heaviest bird traffic for fall migration along these flyways. Out west, Lewis's woodpeckers and golden eagles travel the Pacific Flyway, and the Central Flyway is well known for its huge numbers of sandhill cranes and snow geese, especially in March on the northward journey. The Mississippi Flyway gets big numbers of waterfowl and pelicans as well as colorful prothonotary warblers. The Atlantic Flyway is loaded with warblers like American redstarts and shorebirds like semipalmated sandpipers.

In each of these areas are funneling points, locations where birds tend to congregate as they move through or gather to head in a certain direction. A popular birding activity is to work at these funneling points to count migrating birds; some include the Point Reyes Bird Observatory in California, Kearny in Nebraska, Hawk Ridge in Minnesota, Magee Marsh in Ohio, and Cape May Bird Observatory in New Jersey.

THE NESTING CYCLE

The nesting cycle refers to the process of mating, building a nest, hatching, and rearing young. Survival is a numbers games, and bird species employ many different strategies to survive the odds in the greatest numbers. Geese raise a big batch of eggs all at once. House finches will try to nest as many times as they can in one summer, in some areas producing four to six broods in a season! Eagles raise a small batch of three over several months. Cowbirds put their eggs in someone else's nest and let them do all the work. Every species is different, but all of them have the same goal—getting their genetics into the wild—and to do this success-fully, they must be mindful of territory selection, food sources, and predators.

Courtship and Mating

To find a mate, birds engage in displays and, sometimes, pair bond-ing. For example, oriole males use their flashy plumage and song to announce territory and attract females. Woodcocks vault into the air after sunset and tumble out of the sky, making whistling sounds with their feathers. Woodpeckers can't sing and instead engage in loud drumming to secure the attention of a mate. Great horned owls will cache food and present it as tribute to a female inspecting the territory. Female crows and ravens will give a begging call, per-haps testing a male's attentiveness to feeding chicks. Bald eagles will grab talons and spin down out of the sky. And it's not just males who have to measure up. Spotted sandpiper females give a strutting display up and down shorelines to attract males. There's no one perfect dating strategy that fits all birds.

Some birds take it to the next level and engage in pair bonding (the equivalent of foreplay), like when a male cardinal feeds a female at the feeder, or when birds preen each other by rubbing their bills around their mates' head. Great blue herons will pair up at a nest and try stabbing each other, eventually turning into gentle bill caresses.

Very few birds are truly monogamous. Some birds, like brown-headed cowbirds, will mate with several females. Other birds, like geese, will establish a pair bond and a nest site with a partner. And others, like red-winged blackbirds, will establish pairs but are not above sneaking for a quick copulation with the neighbor.

Building the Nest

Nests aren't so much a home for birds as they are a nursery or crib to raise the babies before they are old enough to fend for themselves. Nests are often tucked away and hidden, far from other bird species. Nests come in all shapes and sizes, from the gigantic stick nests made by birds of prey to the small holes scraped in gravel parking lots to lay eggs (killdeer), the sturdy mud nests constructed on bridges by swallows, and the inexplicable, randomly arranged sticks that serve as nests for pigeons. Some species like woodpeckers require a bit more protection from weather and will excavate cavities in trees in which to raise young. Many species are content to squat in a secondhand woodpecker cavity, including wrens, chickadees, tree swallows, wood ducks, and screech owls.

Sometimes, birds of different species will build communal nests next to one another. Eastern bluebirds and tree swallows will nest side by side, and all the adults will defend the territory together. Herons, egrets, cormorants, and even storks will form giant colonies and tolerate one another as they raise young. If you are one nest out of hundreds, then perhaps you are less likely to be the nest that gets raided by eagles.

From Hatching to Leaving the Nest

Bird embryos develop in eggs outside their mothers' bodies. Laying eggs allows the embryo to develop further, in a hard protective shell, before coming out into the world. It was impractical from an evolutionary standpoint for birds to carry embryos to full development because birds have evolved to fly and carrying an embryo would weigh them down. Different species have evolved to grow at different rates in their eggs, and once they hatch, they often still have some growing to do. An incubation period is how long it takes for the embryo to grow large enough to hatch. American robins have an incubation period of roughly 12 to 14 days and come out of the egg naked and blind. Wood ducks incubate for roughly 30 days, and their young come out of the egg covered in down, open-eyed, and capable of jumping down from as high as 50 feet and running to water.

Young birds go through an awkward phase when learning to fly. This is a dangerous time for them, not only because of predators but also because of well-meaning people. They need to flutter, crash, and fall off perches to learn to fly. If you see a young bird that can't fly well, leave it be unless it is in immediate danger from a cat or is in the middle of the road. The parents are still taking care of it.

As an observer, you'll notice that bird eggs vary in size and color. Some will be spotted, and others could be bright blue. Adult birds usually try to keep a low profile around the nest so as not to attract predators. When you get too close, some birds, such as robins and cardinals, will give angry chip notes or make other harsh calls to teach their young to be wary of humans. If you see a young bird alone, the adult is likely hidden nearby, waiting for you to leave.

Birding Life: Creating a Bird-Friendly Backyard

Once you catch the birding bug, you may start looking for ways to draw birds to you rather than the other way around. A bird-friendly yard starts with a few simple steps.

- Yards with bird-friendly native plants such as oak, sunflower, chokecherries, pine, blazing star, and cone-flower will have the most birds. If everyone planted one native plant in their yard every year, it would contribute significantly to bird conservation.

- Keep cats indoors. North America's birds did not evolve with domestic cats, and domestic cats account in large part for severe bird population declines. Even if a bird escapes the jaws of a cat, it may die of infection within 48 hours.

- Keep feeders clean. If a feeder looks gross to you, it needs to be cleaned with a mild solution of bleach and water. At the very least, clean your feeders once a season, if not once a month. For hummingbirds, rather than using a hummingbird feeder that requires weekly cleaning, attract them with nectar-rich flowers like salvia, bee balm, and cardinal flower.

- Windows kill lots of birds. Dirty windows help prevent collisions. You can also use decals on the outside or periodically mark up your window with a highlighter marker to prevent collisions.

- Ditch the lawns. Manicured grass lawns are essentially a green desert to birds. Allowing clover and dandelions brings in pollinator insects, which make up a large portion of bird diets. You save money by going a bit more natural with your lawn and will spot more birds and wildlife in your yard as a bonus.

- Most birds eat black sunflower seeds. Avoid millet and milo, and if you want cardinals, look for feeders with trays or a wide perching area.

GROOMING

Birds are covered in feathers that need to function around the clock for movement, maintaining body temperature, and communication. Just like we need to take care of our teeth and skin, birds need to take care of their feathers so they stay strong and ready to fly. Birds only groom their feathers when they feel safe and usually in a hidden place. A grooming bird could be an easy target for a passing predator.

Preening

Birds use their beaks to comb through their feathers, similar to the way people use a comb. They zip it over every feather. This practice is known as preening; the preen gland, which sits right above the tail, secretes an oil that the bird spreads to groom its feathers. Birds will squeeze the preen gland with their beak and rub the oil into the feathers or rub their head all over it, using the oils to keep feathers water-resistant.

Water Bathing

Just about all birds use water for bathing when they can find it. In dryer parts of the US, a water feature will fetch you more birds than a bird feeder. Birds get as wet as they can by splashing and ruffling their feathers, and most birds only need very shallow pools of water, like puddles, especially if they are small. Hummingbirds are too small for birdbaths but have been observed zipping through sprinklers to get wet enough for a bath.

Dust Bathing

Loose powdery dirt or fine sand is attractive for many species to bathe in. We aren't entirely sure why birds do this, but most likely dust or sand are more effective than water at getting parasites off the skin and feathers. Some birds are more apt to engage in this behavior than others, particularly house sparrows, quail, and turkeys. Some birds lack a preen gland, so dust bathing is a way to make up for that.

Molting

Feathers get a lot of wear and tear, so periodically birds will molt or shed feathers and grow new ones. Every bird is different. Gold-finches go through a complete molt twice a year. Other birds do it once a year or different feathers every other year. Usually, feathers are gradually shed so a bird doesn't lose all the feathers at once. But most waterfowl lose all their flight feathers at once, rendering them flightless for a few weeks. And some cardinals and blue jays will molt all their head feathers at once, making them resemble miniature vultures.

Outstretched Wings

Outstretched wings signify different grooming techniques for different species. You may see birds like blue jays or robins lying on the ground with their wings stretched out, which could indicate "anting," an activity where birds let ants crawl on their feathers, presumably as a method to remove parasites. You might see larger birds like vultures and cormorants stretching out their wings while perched. In the case of vultures, they're using the sun to shape the contour of their feathers after a long flight. Cormorants are drying their feathers out after swimming and hunting underwater.

Birding Life: Eat Like a Bird

Bird diet is another behavioral factor that helps you iden-tify birds and understand their body and bill shape. For example, birds that eat meat will typically have a curved beak. There are eight predominant categories of bird diet, but keep in mind, most birds are omnivores and eat a com-bination of these diets. Hummingbirds, for example, rely on insects as much as they rely on nectar. Chickadees like seed, but they also like suet in the form of fat deposits found on a deer carcass.

SEED-EATING: Seed-eating birds typically have thick, conical beaks ideal for cracking open hard shells. Cardi-nals, grosbeaks, and sparrows are good examples. You'll see these birds at a bird feeder or where there are trees, grasses, or meadows.

FRUGIVORES: These birds eat fruit primarily and can often be spotted around orchards. Waxwings and catbirds eat quite a bit of fruit when not seeking out insects.

NECTAR-EATING: Hummingbirds fall into this category and need to be where it's warm enough for nectar-rich flowers to bloom. These birds flock to backyards with nectar-rich plants.

INSECTIVORES: Birds that primarily eat insects have thinner beaks, like swallows and warblers.

MEAT-EATING: Meat eaters typically have hooked beaks that they use to rip open flesh. Meat is everywhere for birds like crows, including in our backyards—think mice, rabbits, and squirrels.

CARRION-EATING: Many birds aren't above eating carrion (decaying flesh of dead animals), including bald eagles; magpies and crows will also partake of a carcass. Eagles, ravens, and vultures all enjoy roadkill, and herons are fond of decaying meat in landfills.

FISH-EATING: Fish-eating birds typically have a hooked beak or a sharp, spear-like beak like a heron or kingfisher. These birds gather around bodies of water.

INVERTEBRATE-EATING: These birds can have long beaks for probing, like many shorebirds. You'll find birds searching for food near rivers, streams, sea-sides, and wetlands.

SPEAK LIKE A BIRDER

Like any hobby, birding has its own terms of art. Here are some key terms you might encounter with birders online or out in the wild.

Digiscope *(noun or verb)*
A technique of using a digital camera—whether a single-lens reflex or a smartphone—with a spotting scope or binoculars to take pictures of birds. When used with binoculars, this can sometimes be referred to as "digibinning."

Yes, I have documentation of the rarity; I digiscoped it and added it to my eBird report.

Dipped *(verb)*
When you look for a bird but didn't get it, failed to spot it.

I dipped on the stakeout bird; it was so disappointing.

eBird *(noun)*
The main database birders use to report sightings and look for potential birds. It's free to create an account and use the app to report birds. It is run by the Cornell Lab of Ornithology.

Did you eBird that brant? I'd love to be copied on your checklist so I can have it on my life list, too.

Endemic *(noun)*
A bird that can only be found in one place, usually a country.

The world's smallest hummingbird, the bee hummingbird, is an endemic to Cuba.

Fallout *(noun)*
Birds forced out of the sky due to weather, like storms. They are usually exhausted and searching for food on or low to the ground.

The fallout at South Padre Island Convention Center is so intense; please bring orange halves with you to help try to feed the birds that just crossed the Gulf.

LBJ *(noun)*
Shorthand for "little brown job," which is basically sparrows or any other small warbler. These tend to be frustrating to birders because their muted and indistinguishable markings make them hard to identify.

Yesterday's hike was beautiful but not great birding. We saw plenty of LBJs, but I couldn't identify any of them.

Lifer *(noun)*
A bird that you have never seen before. This is sometimes referred to as a life bird.

Curt ordered chocolate cream pie to celebrate his lifer Kirtland's warbler that he saw for the first time at the Biggest Week in American Birding.

Lister *(noun)*
Most birders keep a life list of the birds that they have seen, but a lister is more intense about finding a new bird to list.

Craig invited Tony to go photograph sandhill cranes at Crex Meadows, but being a true lister, Tony instead headed to Duluth with Jeff to chase the golden-crowned sparrow, which he'd never ticked.

Nemesis *(noun)*
A bird that eludes you. It can be a rarity or a common bird in your state, but no matter how many times you chase it or how many people are there watching it for you, when you arrive it will be gone.

John told Sharon that the spruce grouse are practically guaranteed; he'd seen them every day for a week. But when she arrived at 5:00 a.m. after a five-hour drive, there were none to be seen, so they remained her nemesis bird.

Patagonia Picnic Table Effect *(noun)*
A phrase that refers to an area that is not well birded but suddenly becomes an eBird hot spot because people keep finding good birds there. This phrase has its origins in an actual picnic table in Patagonia where a rare bird once was sighted, drawing a crowd of international birders.

The Patagonia Picnic Table Effect has struck again. Brian had birded the Anoka cemetery his whole life, but after he found a saw-whet owl there, other birders came and soon found red crossbills, northern goshawk, varied thrush, and Townsend's solitaire. It's officially listed as an eBird hot spot.

Patch *(noun)*
A place you bird regularly.

I finally found a dickcissel in my patch.

Peeps *(noun)*
Small shorebirds that are hard to identify.

I suspect I had a western sandpiper in that flock of peeps, but a peregrine flushed it (startled it into flight) before I could confirm.

Pelagic *(adjective)*
A type of birding that takes you out on boats into the ocean to look for seabirds such as petrels, albatross, boobies, and jaegers.

I signed up for one of Debi Shearwater's pelagics and was seasick, but at least I got my lifer Laysan albatross.

Pish *(noun and verb)*
A technique used to get hidden birds to come out. Many birders have strong opinions on how to do it. It's basically saying the word "pish" but in a whisper. Some bird species are very curious about it and will come out of thick patches of dogwood to see what is making the noise.

I just pished up a common yellowthroat and then a sedge wren popped up, too.

Spark bird *(noun)*
This is the first bird that developed someone's interest in watching birds.

My spark bird was the pileated woodpecker. It's the size of a crow.

Stakeout Bird
A rarity bird that has been hanging out in one spot and tracked by birders who report it so that others can come to see the bird.

Oh, that guy? He never finds rarities on his own; he only gets stakeout birds.

Stringer *(noun)*
A person of dubious birding reputation who tends to spot rarities that no one else sees. Their bird reports may also be described as "stringy."

I was going to chase that thick-billed longspur but then saw it was reported by the state's biggest stringer and decided to sleep in instead.

Tick *(noun)*
A bird that you check off on your list.

I ticked the clay-colored sparrow but dipped on grasshopper sparrow today.

Trash bird *(noun)*
An extremely common bird. This is sometimes used as a means of humblebragging when someone reports a rarity for their area.

"Oh, you saw a bald eagle? Yeah, that's a trash bird where I live."

Twitcher *(noun)*
A hard-core birder who will drop everything to get a bird on their list, typically more extreme than a lister. "Twitch" can also be used as a verb.

Joey is such a twitcher, she once canceled a date with Prince so she could go see the first state record of an ivory gull that was four hours away.

Joey missed the meeting because she went to twitch the frigate-bird that was reported on Lake Erie.

TWO BIRDING 101

This chapter will take you into the nitty-gritty of birding: How to get started, what equipment you'll need, how to choose a birding location, how to identify and report birds, and how to get help for tricky identifications. We'll also talk about how to find other birders and what to expect as you join your new flock.

BIRDING EQUIPMENT

With just a few pieces of equipment, your enjoyment of birding can increase exponentially. These suggestions will help you observe and record as well as keep you comfortable and protected while out and about.

Binoculars

The one identifying characteristic of a birder is a pair of binoculars. They are essential for finding and identifying birds.

Binoculars (or binos or bins, to birders) are available in a range of magnifications and lens sizes represented by an equation like 10×50. The first number is the magnification. So, on a 10×50, the image will appear 10 times closer than it does with your naked eye. The second number is the diameter in millimeters of the bottom lens of a binocular. The larger the lens, the clearer the image.

Binoculars can range quite a bit in price, depending on the power of magnification but also the quality of the materials. Most birders go for eight- or 10-power magnification. Keep in mind, higher magnification gives you a closer image of a bird, but the higher you go, the smaller the field of view, which can make finding the bird a challenge. Also, high magnification can pick up any shaking you may have going on, which affects image quality.

I wouldn't recommend a 30-year-old pair found in the back of an uncle's closet, but it is possible to find some great starter binoculars in the $200 to $300 range. Do some field research. Ask birders what brands they use and prefer. When you see birders in person, ask if you can hold and look through their binoculars. Some may feel too wide or too narrow for you. Some may feel too heavy or too small. It is standard for binoculars to come with lifetime warranties, but some companies are better than others when it comes to actual customer service. After asking around and some hands-on research, you'll be ready to take the plunge.

For the serious birder, spotting scopes offer greater magnification. They work especially well for watching waterfowl and other faraway birds like hawks. They are expensive, however, and require carrying a tripod and extra unwieldy equipment in the field.

Hold the Flash: Taking the Perfect Photo

When it comes to identifying or documenting rare birds, cameras are an essential tool. Field notes and sketches can help confirm identification, but they aren't as definitive as a photo. Photography is a great way to get souvenirs as well as document rarities. Digital SLRs (single-lens reflex camera) with a zoom lens are so popular and accessible that some birders forgo binoculars and go out with just the camera. Birds move quickly in the field. If you have a camera, you can get photos and video to help you identify an unknown bird later.

Many birders engage in a technique called digiscoping or phonescoping for their photos and videos, by using a smartphone with a spotting scope. You can purchase special cases for phones to attach them quickly to binoculars or scopes. Because birders carry phones for notes and using eBird anyway, using them for photos instead of a camera works well. The upside to this technique is that scopes and binoculars are waterproof whereas cameras are not. And a phone fits easily in a coat pocket.

A note on flash: Most birds will be too far away for flash, but even if you are close enough, avoid it; many bird species experience flash differently than we do because they have more rods in their eyes.

Clothing

For years, there was a stereotype that birders wore convertible pants, with oversized bird T-shirts, floppy hats, and fishing vests for all their equipment. Nowadays, birders aren't always recognizable by their clothing, and you can dress however you feel comfortable for the occasion. Are you going birding on a warm day in a city park? A sundress or shorts with comfortable sandals could work. If you're headed to a national wildlife refuge or state park, consider moisture-wicking clothing and layers. Do you plan to hike through some marshes or mudflats to look for shorebirds? Consider rubber boots and mosquito netting. If you're worried about ticks, treat your clothing with permethrin the day before you wear it.

Other Essentials

Keeping these items in your birding bag will ensure that you're always prepared:

- Sunscreen
- Water
- Insect repellent
- Snacks
- Pencil and notebook
- Lens-cleaning cloth

- External battery and cable (to keep your phone charged)
- Hand warmers
- Hat
- Rain jacket or poncho

You'll note that a field guide isn't part of this list. Field guides are best studied ahead of time and consulted after your birding trip is over. If you have the guide with you while birding, you risk spending more time looking at the book to ID a bird instead of actually watching an unknown bird.

Birding Life: Getting Techy

We live in an age of wonder as far as accessing information in the field and digitally reporting bird sightings. Here are some of the most useful birding apps:

- **eBird:** A free birding app and database operated by the Cornell Lab of Ornithology. You can report your sightings and learn what birds are being seen around the world. It will even provide driving directions.

- **Merlin:** A free bird identification app that helps you identify birds by question, photo, or even by sound recording.

- **BirdsEye:** This paid app uses eBird to help you find birds near you and offers driving directions to the birds or nearby hot spots.

- There are many field guide apps. Some of the most popular to check out include iBird, Audubon, and Sibley.

IDENTIFYING CHARACTERISTICS

Field marks, color, plumage, and voice are still helpful in identifying birds in the field, but modern birding has shifted focus more to location, season, behavior, and GISS (general impression, size, and shape) as more definitive identifiers. Keep your binoculars on a bird for as long as possible, and take notes either on a pad or the voice memo feature on your phone to document the details.

Habitat/Location or Range

All bets are off during migration, but there are times when you can figure out bird identification based on *where* you saw the bird. If someone told me they saw a hawk nesting in a pine tree and they identified it as a northern harrier, I would call false because harriers nest on the ground in open fields and marshes. Learn where certain birds can be found. You'll soon notice certain species are found together, such as red-winged blackbirds and common yellowthroats.

Season

Because birds migrate, season is an identifying factor that goes hand in hand with location. Spotting a junco in Indiana in January is typical. Finding one there in July would be rare. If you consider location and migration patterns, season can be the missing piece in a correct identification, even if you have a clear view of your bird.

Behavior

Behavior is integral to identification, even something as simple as the way it flies. Suppose you see a large black bird in the sky and you are not sure if it is a raven or a crow. Ravens soar in circles like a hawk or eagle, but crows cannot do this. Consider another example. Spotted sandpipers only have spots on their bellies during breeding season, but you can always identify these birds because they bob their butts up and down.

Shape

Shape is also a major help when identifying birds. Some birds are very round, some are sleek. Warblers and vireos are essentially the same size, but you'll start to notice that vireos have a more horizontal shape and thicker beak than warblers. Flight shape can be key to identification. Red-tailed hawks have long broad wings and a shorter tail in relation to their chunkier bodies. Cooper's hawks are sleek, with short wings and long tails. Note shape as much as you note color when you see a new bird.

Group

As you bird, you'll begin to notice that certain groups share physical and vocal characteristics even when they are not in the same species. Cardinals and rose-breasted grosbeaks are chunky birds with thick, conical beaks. Purple martins and tree swallows are not the same species, but they both nest in cavities, fly around swallowing insects, and have a similar shape. As you learn your birds, study how different species can look and behave similarly.

Field Marks

These are characteristics referenced in field guides that are specific to a certain bird. Field marks include items like eye-rings, stripes, and wing bars, a subtle dark comma-like mark visible only when the bird flies. While field marks are still important, modern birding has shifted its identification focus more to location, season, behavior, and shape.

Color

Bird color (on their feathers and elsewhere) helps in identification but is not always reliable. Goldfinches, bright yellow in spring and summer, molt into a dull olive in winter. Male indigo buntings are brilliant blue in full sun but can look almost black in the shade. Color is a guide but not always a clincher when it comes to identification.

Plumage

Feather size, shape (including the tail and head feathers), and color can help you with identification. Did you see a large chunky bird startle from a road with a long, pointed tail? That tail will mean it was a pheasant and not a grouse. Did you detect what you thought was a large brown owl, but you were able to hear it flap? That was more likely a hawk because owl feathers are bristled, making them almost silent when they fly.

Voice

Learning bird songs and sounds is a bit like learning a second language. Birds sing, give chip notes (a single note that often sounds like "chip"), make specific sounds for predators, and even have different "dialects" throughout the United States. A house finch in New York won't sound quite the same as a house finch in California. Young birds have to practice their songs in the fall and sometimes sound nothing at all like the adults. Some birds are even mimics, so if you suddenly hear a killdeer way out of season, it could be a starling doing an accurate imitation. As you learn, focus on the birds you do know. Each season, try to learn three new bird songs instead of trying to learn them all at once.

Size

Size does matter when identifying a bird, but it is one of the things new birders often get wrong. Downy and hairy woodpeckers look almost identical to each other except the hairy is almost twice the size. If you've not seen a hairy before, however, a large downy could fool you. In Cooper's hawks, females are noticeably larger than males. You might see a female that is closer in size to a crow and a male closer in size to a blue jay. Keep size in mind, but don't be married to it. Like people, individual birds can vary in size.

Putting It Together

Picture yourself birding at a small creek in May in northern Wisconsin. You spy an LBJ (little brown job) while walking along the creek. You become anxious because so many birds are small and brown. But then you start noticing everything: It's feeding along a stream, it's brown but has streaks on the belly, it is constantly pumping its backside up and down. You start to narrow it down but then determine that this pumping behavior means it's not a sparrow, but a waterthrush. You know that there are two types of waterthrush in the United States. But you are in northern Wisconsin, where Louisiana waterthrushes don't breed. It's a safe bet that this is a northern waterthrush.

Birding Life 101: Misidentification

Remember, every birder misidentifies a bird. In fact, some of us will do it very publicly. It happens.

When you are a new birder, be prepared for people to question an identification of a bird that is out of range or rare. This happens with eBird reports, too. Try to avoid reading these posts in an angry tone and read them with a friendly voice . . . or even an Elmer Fudd voice. When you report what might be considered an unusual bird, have your notes and photos ready. Even a video of a bird on a smartphone can help solidify identity, especially if you captured the bird's call. Do not take questions personally; there are many common mistakes made by new birders, and most experienced birders want to help.

IN THE FIELD

The great thing about birding is that you can do it anywhere. These tips and tricks will help you plan, maximize your time, and increase your chances of finding birds.

Finding Your Path

Birding can be a simple or as complex as you would like. Most people start birding in their backyards; maybe they notice a red-bellied woodpecker for the first time and then join a Facebook group to learn more. From there you may see a specific park mentioned a lot and head in that direction. Another place to start is with eBird. You can find your county and look for "hot spots." These are areas that attract many birders and have had many sightings submitted to the database. Some apps, such as Audubon and BirdsEye, will help you pick out nearby birding locations and give you driving directions on your smartphone.

As helpful as apps and websites can be, however, nothing can replace firsthand knowledge. Ask other birders or type into a search engine "How to bird [and then select your location of interest, like River Migratory Bird Refuge]." You may find sites and blogs of people who bird the area and are anxious to share the information. You can also join Facebook and other online birding groups and ask your questions as well. Before you know it, you'll be visiting sewage lagoons for shorebirds and ducks or signing up for a birding tour company to visit the Arctic Circle and see all three species of eider.

How Not to Wing It

You will have a much better bird-watching experience with a plan in place. Set an alarm; be out the door early in the morning. The early birder gets the birds, so to speak. There's a lull that happens around noon and lasts until late afternoon; birds just aren't as active in midday.

Know what birds you are hoping to see. Map out your location and route. Know where trailheads are located and what the parking situations are like. Are you birding in an urban area? Chances are good you may have to pay for metered parking. Are you going to finally hit that national wildlife refuge everyone raves about? Make sure to check the website for closures, especially in and around hunting seasons. Sometimes when a rarity is present, the bird may only show at a certain time of day, so get the intel from other birders.

Make sure you understand the terrain and if it fits with your abilities. Many hawk watching sites have excellent trails to explore, but they may be on high bluffs. Some scientific and natural areas do not allow you to go off trail, but other parks have wilderness trails only. Could the trails be underwater? Be prepared with supplies for the duration.

Bird Calls: Spotting by Sound

The birders with the longest lists are the ones who know their bird calls. You don't have to know every bird call, but if you know the common ones, you'll be prepared when a new one pops up so you can be on the lookout for the new bird.

A great bird to learn is the American robin. Once you start with that bird, you'll soon realize that other bird songs sound similar. Tanagers sound like a robin with a frog in its throat; grosbeaks sound like a professionally singing robin.

You can also start to pick up on how birds in the same genus can have a type of sound. For example, wrens are very chattery. Once you get used to what a house wren sounds like in your backyard, for instance, you may notice a chattery bird in marshes that sounds similar but not quite the same as what you hear in your yard; this could be a marsh wren or a sedge wren.

Birders will sometimes use mnemonic devices to describe the rhythm of a bird's call. Here are some popular clues:

▸ Where are my keys! (red-winged blackbird)

▸ Who cooks for you? (barred owl)

- Pee-pee, I have to pee! (brown creeper)

- If I could seize one, I would squeeze one and I'd squeeze till it squirts! (warbling vireo)

Clue into the attitude that birds have when they make noise as well. More birders find hidden owls and hawks by paying attention to other angry bird sounds. Some birds, such as the American robin, don't even sound like themselves when they give their high-pitched slurred whistle that alerts everyone to a Cooper's hawk. Some birds, such as the merlin, will silence all the birds in your yard when they blast through. Many screech owls, saw-whet owls, and boreal owls have been located by birders listening to angry chickadees making repetitive "dee dee dee" notes.

10 Rules of Birding

Here are my top 10 recommendations for new birders.

1. Give birds their space and a chance to get used to your presence. Birds are generally wary of humans. If a bird is staring at you, you have its attention, and it's likely to fly away.

2. Don't trespass. Just don't. You'll be tempted, but it makes private landowners angry, and in the case of businesses and government sites, it can cause them to close off a good birding area entirely.

3. Avoid playback. Playing recorded calls of birds in the field can be useful for drawing out birds, but it can also be annoying—to the birds and to fellow birders. Use discretion.

4. Don't ask for owl roosting or nesting locations. Owls are cool to see and challenging to find but are also uniquely vulnerable. Unlike other birds, they have a tendency to sit in one spot, allowing humans to closely approach them. If

they do flush because someone approached too close, they may have lost a valuable meal, they can be vulnerable to birds that don't like them, or they may fly in a panic toward a street and get hit by a car.

5. Leave baby birds alone: 99.9 percent of the baby birds found on the ground are learning to fly, and they need those critical few days to flutter around and learn the basics and what a predator is. Unless that baby bird is in immediate danger from a cat, leave it alone.

6. Don't get mad at eBird reviewers. People will question your rare or unusual bird sightings. They will attempt to do it as politely as they know how. It's not anything personal; it's a clarification of information.

7. If you feed birds, keep it tidy. Keep your bird feeders clean. Dirty feeders help spread disease and will undo any of the good done by providing food.

8. Plant one native plant in your yard a year. If everyone took the time to plant one native plant in their yard every year, that would do more to help birds than any bird feeders. Native plants can provide seeds and berries, attract insects that birds like to eat, and provide places for birds to hide or nest.

9. Be aware of your surroundings. Avoid standing in front of people who might be trying to find a bird. Nothing is more annoying than when you're focusing on a bird and someone plants themself in front of your scope.

10. Share your bird sightings. When you're starting out, you learn where to find birds from other birders. Putting your birding list in systems like eBird helps out other birders and contributes to science.

Birding Life: Pish Off

Pishing is whispering the word "pish" to attract birds; everyone has a different way of doing it. You'll witness many birders using the technique, especially in spring and summer.

There are a few different theories as to why birds will come check out pishing. One theory is that it sounds like baby birds begging for food, and adult birds in breeding season are preprogrammed to respond to calls for feeding. Another theory is that it sounds like a bird mobbing a predator, so other birds want to join in the mob or check out what the danger is.

LOGGING AND SUBMITTING YOUR BIRD SIGHTINGS

The most commonly used platform for documenting sightings is eBird. Entries in eBird help researchers around the world better understand bird populations, movement, and breeding ranges. Take photos and take as many notes as you can after watching the bird. The most important things to note are location, time of year, type of habitat, markings like the presence and number of wing stripes, and bird behavior.

Crafting Your Entry

Before eBird and photography changed the landscape of birding, people had to write up their sightings for the sightings to be considered valid. You might still need this technique in a pinch. Here is a list of what to include:

- ▸ Date and time of sighting

- ▸ Location

- ▸ Description of habitat

- ▸ Color and size of the bird

Include any distinguishing marks such as wing bars, hoods, spots, three main colors, head shape, tail length, whether when perched the wings went beyond the tail. Include behaviors like methods of flapping or soaring. Did it hop or run on the ground, or did it stay still? Did it bob up and down or pump its tail? Was it feeding? What was it eating?

Some people even try to include a sketch, no matter how crude.

Sketching Your Bird

With the availability of digital cameras, not as many people sketch in the field anymore. But if you are desperate to report a rare bird and you don't have a camera or the batteries died, sketching can help. You don't have to be great at it; I know someone in Florida who documented a rarity with the colors in a makeup palette they had with them.

Focus on the overall shape, the beak, the tail, any marks such as spots, wing bars, and eyelines—anything that you see right there in the moment. Don't worry about your artistic ability.

FINDING YOUR FLOCK

Some birders like to keep it social and fun, and others prefer to bird alone and enjoy the solitude of nature. There's something to be said for finding more birds when you aren't busy chatting with a friend. Still, don't miss out on becoming a part of the birding community. It is far easier to find other birders now than it was when I was growing up in the 1980s in Indiana. There are local bird clubs, Facebook groups, Twitter hashtags, old-school email Listservs, bar gatherings called Birds and Beers or Birds and Brews, WhatsApp groups, the sky is the limit. You might also consider checking with local nature centers to see if they offer bird walks. Find out from other birders if there is a local chat group that shares sightings. Many states offer birding festivals, and you can visit your local fest to connect with local birders there.

I live in Minnesota, and we have a general Minnesota Birding group and offshoots like Minnesota Birding Light, Minnesota Birding Photographers, and Minnesota County Listers; there are even multiple groups just looking at owls. Just about every state has similar clubs and resources for birders, so you'll have no shortage of people to answer any just-starting-out questions that pop up.

HOW TO USE THIS FIELD GUIDE

Most field guides are organized by taxonomy, but we are bucking that trend. This one is organized by types of birds. In fact, the book uses a color-coded tab system to help you easily turn to the types of birds you're seeking:

- **Yellow:** Common backyard birds
- **Green:** Songbirds (park birds)
- **Blue:** Waterbirds, shorebirds, waterfowl
- **Red:** Raptors and birds of prey

This book features just 150 of the more than 900 birds you can find in the United States, but it's meant to get you started and whet your appetite. Entries include photos and information on location, size, shape, color, field marks, behavior, and any distinctions between males and females. When you find a bird that's not in this book, you are no longer a beginner, and you are ready for a more extensive field guide. Entries also include habitat icons. Keep in mind, though, that you will find some birds in more than one habitat:

 Wave icon means the bird lives near water.

 Tree icon means the bird lives in the forest or open woodlands.

 Grass icon means the bird lives in flat plains and grasslands.

 Shrub icon means the bird lives in short, dense foliage, including in urban areas.

Now it's time to begin your birding adventure. You'll start out in chapter 3 with the most common birds you'll see, which may give you a chance to practice your skills in your own backyard.

THREE COMMON BACKYARD BIRDS

A soft-brown-and-gray dove with a long pointy tail, this bird is known for a mournful "hoo-ing" call. It's typically found around farms and suburban backyards or perched on wires. When mourning doves fly, they make a unique whistling sound as they flap.

COLOR: Soft brown and gray

HEAD: Tiny head with an eye that looks like it's apologizing

GISS: The shape and size of a tennis ball, with a long pointy tail

RANGE: The US and Canada

DID YOU KNOW . . .

Mourning doves have a large crop off their esophagus to store seeds they've consumed. In the first few days after their chicks hatch from the egg, the adults feed them a secretion from the crop called "crop milk" or "pigeon milk." Morning doves build flimsy nests out of twigs on just about anything from old nests made by other birds, light fixtures, boxes, cactus, or thin branches. It's amazing that the young are able to survive such a thin structure.

ROCK PIGEON *(rok pidg-ion)*

This chunky bird comes in a variety of colors, like gray, black, white, and rusty with hints of purple. They are fast fliers on pointed wings. Their ability to eat anything, from seed to vomit, makes them highly adaptable to remote cliffs, major urban areas, and many places in between. Research shows that one way pigeons navigate is using the Earth's magnetic field.

COLOR: Generally gray but can be black, white, and rust

HEAD: Small head with big eyes that make them look confused

GISS: The shape and size of a softball

RANGE: The US and Canada

EURASIAN COLLARED-DOVE
(YOU-ray-shan coll-r-ed-duh-v)

These are large off-white birds with a black neck band and bright white undertail tip. Look for them in suburbs and agricultural areas perched on wires or roof tops. They were introduced to the Bahamas in the 1970s and worked their way into the US, where they have been ever since.

COLOR: White with black accents

HEAD: Round with a thin beak

GISS: The shape and size of a softball

RANGE: Widespread in the US

BROWN-HEADED COWBIRD
(brow-n hed-ed k-ow-bird)

Males are black with a green iridescent sheen on the body and a completely brown head with a black conical bill. Females and young cowbirds look like large sparrows with their brownish-gray bodies and streaking on the belly. Some show a light chin patch under a conical bill. Females will lay eggs in any nest they can find, leaving the young cowbirds to be raised by birds often smaller than they are.

COLOR: Black, brown, and gray

HEAD: Rounded with dark conical bill

GISS: The shape of a submarine and the size of a softball

RANGE: Widespread in North America

FEMALE

MALE

EUROPEAN STARLING
(You-roe-pee-an star-ling)

In summer, starlings are iridescent black with a greenish-purple sheen and yellow bill. In winter, they are dark with white spots on their feathers, and their bills turn black. Young starlings are gray and noisy. Starlings have soft, insectivore beaks that make it impossible for them to eat seeds with a hard shell like black-oil sunflower or safflower. Large winter flocks of starlings are known as murmurations. You'll find them in meadows, farms, near water, or in urban areas.

COLOR: Black, white, and gray

HEAD: Flat with a longish beak

GISS: Shaggy, the shape and size of a tennis ball

RANGE: Widespread in North America

SUMMER   WINTER

RED-WINGED BLACKBIRD
(red-wing-ed bl-ack-bird)

Males are all black with a red shoulder patch, bordered by a yellow line. The patch is not always visible; males can conceal it to keep the peace while in large flocks. The patch is to attract females during breeding. Females fool many sparrows by being brown and streaky and resembling a large sparrow. Red-winged blackbirds are typically found near water, where they nest, or in large fields looking for grain and insects.

COLOR: Black and brown

HEAD: Round, with a sharp, conical beak

GISS: The shape of a cigar and the size of a tennis ball

RANGE: Widespread in North America

MALE

FEMALE

COMMON GRACKLE *(comm-on grak-kel)*

This dark, iridescent blackbird with a bronze sheen on the body and dark blue head with a long tail has distinct yellow eyes and a long, pointed dark bill. Young grackles are gray and noisy. Grackles eat many insects but will take over a bird feeding station during migration and the breeding season.

COLOR: Dark bronze, blue, and gray

HEAD: Dark with yellow eye with a sharp bill

GISS: The shape of a cigar, with a noticeable tail

RANGE: Widespread in eastern and central North America

GREAT-TAILED GRACKLE
(gray-tail-ed grak-kel)

Males are an iridescent bluish purple with yellow eyes, pointed beak, and enormously long tail. Females are brown and darker on the back and paler on their underside, and have yellow eyes. Great-tailed grackles are known for giant, loud roosts in urban areas with thousands of birds gathering on power lines or perched in shrubs.

COLOR: Dark blue, purple, and brown

HEAD: Round, with a large pointed beak

GISS: The shape and size of a cigar, with a long tail

RANGE: Southwestern US and expanding

AMERICAN CROW
(Ah-mer-i-can kr-ow)

Smaller than ravens and lacking their ability to soar, these all-black birds have a very sleek look and a higher-pitched call. In the winter, crows will form roosts with thousands of birds coming from miles around. They are as at home in urban areas as they are in rural farmland. If you hear a crow that sounds like it inhaled helium and you're on the East Coast, it could be a fish crow.

COLOR: Black

HEAD: Flat with a thick, pointed black beak

GISS: The size of a volleyball, but sleeker in shape

RANGE: Widespread in North America

COMMON RAVEN *(comm-on ray-van)*

This highly adaptable bird can be found in many places, ranging from the north woods of Minnesota to San Francisco Bay. Large and black, they can be distinguished from crows by their giant beaks, beard-like feathers under the beaks, wedge-shaped tail, ability to soar like hawks, and deep, throaty calls.

COLOR: Black

HEAD: Big and bearded with a giant beak

GISS: Shaggy, the shape and size of a cinder block

RANGE: The middle and western United States and Canada

HOUSE SPARROW *(haus spare-oh)*

Most of the time when you see a small brown bird, it will be the house sparrow, especially in urban and farm settings. House sparrows shift through many shades of brown throughout the year as they molt. Generally, males are dark brown on back, gray underneath with a black chin and bib. Females are paler with mottled gray and brown on back, a buff eyebrow and a pale beak. House sparrows have a notch on their beaks with which they sometimes kill other birds (wrens, bluebirds, chickadees); cavity-nesting, the sparrow will then take over the nest of the dead bird or even nest on its corpse.

COLOR: Brown with gray

HEAD: Small round head, a pale thick, conical beak

GISS: Bouncy, the shape and size of a Ping-Pong ball

RANGE: Widespread in North America

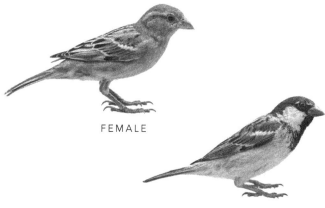

FEMALE

MALE

NORTHERN CARDINAL
(north-urn CAR-di-nal)

This flashy bird is a staple in backyards in the east. Males are distinctive with their bright red bodies, and the females sport brown bodies with hints of red. Young male cardinals resemble females but have black beaks. In late summer, some cardinals molt all the feathers off their heads, revealing black skin. These birds prefer urban yards with thick bushes.

COLOR: Red and brown

HEAD: Crested, triangular with a large conical orange beak

GISS: Round

RANGE: The eastern US

MALE

FEMALE

BLUE JAY *(blew j-ae)*

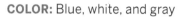

Loud and boisterous, blue jays are beautiful bright blue birds with white spots on the back, dynamic crests, white faces with black accents, gray bellies, and long tails. They can mimic the sounds of other birds and will often mimic the sounds of hawks before flying toward a bird feeder, presumably to scare off other birds. They are typically found where there are oak trees; they often feed on acorns.

COLOR: Blue, white, and gray

HEAD: Crested, masked, dark beak

GISS: The shape and size of a tennis ball, with a tail

RANGE: Widespread in eastern US

DID YOU KNOW . . .

Blue jays are typically found around oak trees and are responsible for planting many acorns when they store them under leaves for use later. During summer and fall blue jays will grab as many seeds as they can and store them in their crops to hide for storage. The migration of blue jays is not completely understood. Hundreds of birds can be seen moving in the spring and fall, but bird banding records show that some birds stay put.

STELLER'S JAY *(Stell-are's j-ae)*

A gorgeous dark jay that can be highly variable in color depending on location. Generally, it has a black head, crest, and back with bright azure blue body and tail. But in parts of their range, the crests and backs can be blue as well. Typically found in mature pine forests, they are excellent mimics of other birds, cats, and dogs.

COLOR: Black and blue

HEAD: Round, with a moveable crest and a long, pointed beak

GISS: The shape and size of a tennis ball, with a tail

RANGE: The western US and Canada

CHICKADEE *(chick-ah-DEE)*

There are seven species of chickadee in North America; the most common are black-capped and Carolina chickadees, which look identical. Most people can only tell them apart by song. These little fluffs of energy have black caps and bibs with white cheeks on a gray body and white belly. They are cavity-nesting birds, found anywhere there are trees.

COLOR: Black, white, and gray

HEAD: Round with stubby black beak

GISS: Round, fluffy, the shape and size of a Ping-Pong ball, with a tail

RANGE: Widespread in North America

TUFTED TITMOUSE *(tuff-ted TIT-maus)*

Five species of titmouse call North America home, with the most common being the tufted titmouse. These sassy little birds have pale gray bodies, accented by large black eyes, an expressive crest, and peach flanks on a white belly. These bold birds will fly down to sleeping pets to pluck out loose hair to line their nests. They are woodland birds that can be found in urban yards with lots of trees.

COLOR: Pale gray and white

HEAD: Large black eye, expressive crest, short black beak

GISS: The shape and size of Ping-Pong ball, with a long tail

RANGE: The eastern US

WHITE-BREASTED NUTHATCH
(why-te-bress-ted NUT-hat-ch)

Four species of nuthatches are found in the United States, with the nasal-sounding white-breasted nuthatch being the most common found year-round. They are noticeable for their habit of hitching down trunks facefirst with their rumps up. If you ever notice a smaller version in winter with a bright rusty underbelly, that is its cousin the red-breasted nuthatch.

COLOR: Gray, black, and white

HEAD: Flat with a dark, pointy beak

GISS: The shape and size of a bar of soap, horizontal

RANGE: The US and Canada

DOWNY WOODPECKER
(dow-nee wood-pek-her)

This is a small black-and-white woodpecker about the size of a sparrow. Males sport a red patch on the backs of their heads and females do not. Named for the downy feathers that surround the short bill, these birds are common guests at feeders, seeking out nuts and suet. In the spring, these birds use short bursts of rapid drumming with their beaks instead of singing to attract mates and signal territory.

COLOR: Black and white

HEAD: Round with a short pointed bill

GISS: Small, the shape and size of an ice-cream cone

RANGE: The US and Canada

DID YOU KNOW . . .

The smallest woodpecker in North America, downy woodpeckers join "mixed flocks" of chickadees, titmice, and nuthatches in winter. The theory is that more birds help find more sources of food. Being small, downy woodpeckers can find food in smaller crevices. They also will forage for water in unique ways, including clinging to melting icicles and using their long tongues to get to flower nectar.

HAIRY WOODPECKER *(bare-ee wood-pek-her)*

A larger version of the downy woodpecker, this bird is noticeable for its longer beak. Birds are black and white with males sporting two small red spots on the back of the head. Females do not have the red marks. Hairy woodpeckers have been known to feed at hummingbird feeders and to sip sap from tree wells drilled by sapsuckers.

COLOR: Black and white

HEAD: Long, pointed beak

GISS: The shape and size of an ice-cream cone

RANGE: The US and Canada

FEMALE

MALE

Males are raspberry red on the head, chest, and flanks, with no brown streaking, unlike the similar house finch. They are also brown on back with a thick, conical bill. Females are white with heavy brown streaks and a bold white eyebrow. During breeding season, these birds are in the woods. In winter, they can be found in many urban and suburban yards. These birds are one of the species of birds that mimics other types of birds, which confuses birders.

COLOR: Raspberry red, brown, and white

HEAD: Round with a large beak

GISS: The shape of a Ping-Pong ball, slightly chunkier in size

RANGE: The US and Canada

FEMALE

MALE

HOUSE FINCH *(haus fin-ch)*

House finches love to nest in hanging plant baskets. Males are streaked brown and white and doused in pink from their heads to their chests. The color comes from their diets, which contain carotenoids in seeds, flowers, and various fruits. Females are heavily streaked brown and white. House finches are susceptible to a type of pink eye and sometimes show up with swollen eyes.

COLOR: White, brown, and pink

HEAD: Round with a thick beak

GISS: The shape and size of a Ping-Pong ball

RANGE: The US and southern Canada

MALE

FEMALE

AMERICAN GOLDFINCH
(Ah-mer-i-can gold-fin-ch)

In summer, male American goldfinches are bright yellow with a black cap, black wings with white wing bars, and a black tail. Females are gray with a yellow and olive wash, black wings, and blondish wing bars. In winter, both are dull brownish yellow with dark wings and buff wing bars. They are quite nomadic in winter, and it's not uncommon for a large flock to disappear for a few weeks in search of food. They live in urban settings, grassy fields, or near water.

COLOR: Yellow, black, and gray

HEAD: Small, round, dainty, pointed beak

GISS: The shape and size of a Ping-Pong ball

RANGE: Widespread in the US

MALE

FEMALE

LESSER GOLDFINCH
(less-er gold-fin-ch)

Male lesser goldfinches have black caps (a little dot on the top of the head) with yellow chins, chest, and bellies. Their backs can vary from black to olive with white patches on the wings and tail. Females are dull yellowish and darker on the back than on their underside. Unlike the American goldfinch, they do not molt into a winter plumage. They like open areas and scrub and hang out near water. Strict vegetarians, they enjoy just about any seed in the sunflower family.

COLOR: Yellow, black, and olive

HEAD: Small with a dainty, conical beak

GISS: The shape and size of a Ping-Pong ball

RANGE: The western US

FEMALE

MALE

PINE SISKIN *(pie-n sis-kin)*

This erratic species can outnumber the most common birds at your feeder but will not show up every year because they are very nomadic. Siskins are tiny and heavily streaked with yellow patches visible on the wings. They typically will cling to, or hang on the side of, any finch feeder in your yard when they show up. Pine siskins are early nesters; when it is very cold out, the female will not leave the nest and the male will feed her while she incubates the eggs.

COLOR: Gray, black, and yellow

HEAD: Round, small, pointed beak

GISS: The shape and size of a Ping-Pong ball

RANGE: Widespread in the US but very nomadic

DARK-EYED JUNCO *(dark-ide junk-o)*

Frequently referred to as "snow birds" because they tend to appear in winter, dark-eyed juncos vary in color regionally. Some birds are all dark gray with white bellies, and others sport a dark hood with brown backs and white bellies, plus a host of colors in between. Watch for them to kick around looking for seeds under a feeder. Juncos nest on the ground in heavily wooded areas.

COLOR: Gray, white, and brown

HEAD: Dark with a tiny, light-colored beak

GISS: The shape and size of a Ping-Pong ball, with a tail

RANGE: Widespread in the US and Canada

WHITE-THROATED SPARROW
(why-te throw-ted spare-oh)

These brown birds can have gray on half their faces, their chests, bellies, and mixed in on their backs. Other birds have tan and brown striping and an off-white chin. Color morphs appear in both sexes. They are noticeable for their habit of kicking the ground looking for seeds under a bird feeder. These birds are found in open areas; habitats can range from scrub in Texas to the taiga of Denali National Park.

COLOR: Brown, gray, tan, and black

HEAD: Striping and small conical beak

GISS: The shape and size of a Ping-Pong ball

RANGE: Widespread in most of the US and Canada

TAN MORPH

BRIGHT MORPH

WHITE-CROWNED SPARROW
(why-te cr-ow-ned spare-oh)

This sassy little gray sparrow has bold black and white stripes on the head and a distinctive pale orange beak. Males and females look alike. Young birds resemble adults but have gray-and-tan striping over the forehead. During breeding season, June through August, they have a unique song that sounds like they are saying, "I'm frickin' everywhere!"

COLOR: Gray

Head: Black and white with pale orange beak

GISS: The shape and size of a Ping-Pong ball

RANGE: Widespread in North America

JUVENILE   ADULT

EASTERN PHOEBE *(EE-stern fee-bee)*

Phoebes are dark gray upright birds with black faces, white chins and bellies, and a habit of pumping their tails when perched. They get their name from their call, which sounds like they are saying, "Feeee bee, feee breeep." Phoebes like to build their nests under the eaves of houses.

COLOR: Gray and white

HEAD: Round with a small, flat beak

GISS: The shape of a submarine and the size of a tennis ball

RANGE: The eastern US and most of Canada

GRAY CATBIRD *(gr-a KAT-bird)*

This gray bird skulks around and mimics the sounds of other birds but will mew like a cat when it feels threatened. Dark gray with a black cap and a rusty patch just under a long tail, catbirds eat insects and fruit and will come to bird feeders that have oranges, mealworms, and suet. They like to hang out low and appreciate very thick cover, like a bush or marsh vegetation.

COLOR: Dark gray

HEAD: Round, dark cap

GISS: The shape of a submarine and the size of a tennis ball

RANGE: Widespread in the US

NORTHERN MOCKINGBIRD
(nor-thurn mahk-ing-bird)

Slender gray birds with long black tails with white stripes on either side, mockingbirds are light gray on top with an off-white chin and belly. They have two white wing bars and a bold patch of white visible in flight. Mockingbirds will mimic the sounds of other birds around them and even pick up mechanical sounds such as car alarms. They love open areas with low, shrubby plants and trees.

COLOR: Gray, black, and white

HEAD: Round with a long, dark beak

GISS: The shape and size of a tennis ball, with a tail, but on the thin side

RANGE: Widespread in southern and eastern US

AMERICAN ROBIN
(Ah-mer-i-can rahb-inn)

This year-round resident spends summers foraging on lawns for insects and winters in tree branches looking for berries or on the water's edge looking for invertebrates. Brownish-gray on the back with an orange belly, females tend to be paler than males. Young

robins have spotted chests when they are learning to fly.

COLOR: Brownish-gray and orange

HEAD: Round, yellow beak

GISS: The shape of a submarine and the size of a tennis ball

RANGE: Widespread in North America

VARIED THRUSH *(var-reed thr-uh-sh)*

Male varied thrushes are gray on the back with an orange belly. They boast a prominent black ring around the chest, and an orange eyebrow with some gray along the flanks. Females are a paler version of the male. In the winter, many birds head farther east than range maps in books suggest. They tend to favor old-growth woods.

COLOR: Gray, orange, and black

HEAD: Horizontal oval with a thin, pointed beak

GISS: The shape and size of a tennis ball

RANGE: The western US and Canada

HOUSE WREN *(haus REN)*

This small boisterous bird will sing its head off all summer. Tiny and many shades of brown, it's known for keeping its tail popped up straight in the air. The back is brown with gray-and-white spotting, it has a buff (light yellow-tan) eyebrow, and light brown belly. House wrens make nests in any cavity they can find in their territory, including wood duck boxes, which are common bird-houses you can purchase at a bird store.

COLOR: Brown

HEAD: Thin, slightly downward-curving bill

GISS: Delicate, tiny, the shape and size of a dust bunny

RANGE: The US, southern Canada, and Mexico

EASTERN BLUEBIRD *(ee-stern blew-bird)*

There are three species of bluebird in North America: eastern, western, and mountain. Male eastern bluebirds are sky blue on the back with an orange belly. Females are a paler version with some gray mixed in. When a male eastern bluebird has decided he likes a birdhouse, he will leave a blade of grass inside to stake his claim.

COLOR: Sky blue, orange, and gray

HEAD: Round with a flat, thin beak

GISS: The shape and size of a tennis ball

RANGE: The US

DID YOU KNOW . . .

Bluebirds are cavity-nesting birds; they naturally use old woodpecker holes but have adapted to use nest boxes that have a hole that is an inch and a half in diameter. They nest alongside tree swallows and black-capped chickadees, and the birds will defend the territory from intruders together. Bluebirds will eat fruit and insects and some people can get them to come to tray feeders by offering live mealworms, dried berries, or suet dough crumbled into bite-size pieces.

TREE SWALLOW *(tr-EE swah-loh)*

This cavity-nesting bird will often nest along with bluebirds in bird-houses or nesting boxes in your backyard. Greenish blue on back (females are duller) and white on the belly, they look like little killer whales when you see their heads poking out of a birdhouse hole. Tree swallows have pointed wings and a short, forked tail. In the western US, there is a similar swallow called a violet-green swallow but is greener than the tree swallow and has a bold white cheek patch that goes up and over the eye.

COLOR: Dark blue, green, and white

HEAD: Like an orca with a short beak

GISS: The shape of a fat cigar, with pointy wings

RANGE: The US

BARN SWALLOW *(bar-nn swah-low)*

These elegant birds fly around grabbing insects in the air. They have dark blue backs, orange bellies, and a long, forked tail. Barn swallows build mud nests and especially like to build them on the eaves of a house or on a porch.

COLOR: Dark blue and orange

HEAD: Round with a small, thin beak

GISS: The shape and size of a cigar, with a forked tail

RANGE: Widespread in the US and Canada

NORTHERN FLICKER *(nor-thurn FLIK-her)*

This is a weird woodpecker that spends more time foraging (and pecking) on the ground than in trees. A large brown bird with dark spots, birds in the east reveal yellow flashing (meaning the colors that are on display when the bird flaps its wings) in flight, and birds in the west flash red. Males are distinguished by their mustaches, which look black in the east and red in the west. Flickers will perch in the tops of trees giving out their loud "wika-wika-wika" calls.

COLOR: Light brown with accents

HEAD: Large head, long dark beak that curves downward, mustache on males

GISS: Chunky, the shape of a softball, with a wide tail

RANGE: Widespread in North America

MALE

FEMALE

CHIMNEY SWIFT *(chem-nee s-wif-t)*

Chimney swifts are cigar-shaped gray birds that practice frenetic wing flapping. They are rarely sighted perched. They fly nonstop, grabbing insects as they go. Chimney swifts are localized to populated areas with open chimneys, which they need for nesting.

COLOR: Dark gray

HEAD: Small, round with a very small, flat beak

GISS: The shape and size of a cigar

RANGE: Urban areas in the US

CEDAR WAXWING *(see-dare wacks-wing)*

These sleek birds typically hang out anywhere there are fruit-bearing trees. Waxwings are a soft brown with a bright yellow tail tip, red waxlike tips on the feathers, a black beak, and an elegant black mask around the eyes. They typically fly around in flocks looking for fruit or insects.

COLOR: Brown with accents of black and yellow

HEAD: Crested, mask, black beak

GISS: The shape and size of a cigar, with a small crest

RANGE: The US and Canada

Males have a rufous (reddish-brown) body and red chin. Sometimes they will have green on the back, but they always show rust among the green. Females are green on back, with a spotty chin and rusty sides. Highly territorial even during migration, they chase off any other hummingbird at flowers or a feeder in what they have decided is "their" yard.

COLOR: Overall rusty with hints of green

HEAD: Small with a long, thin bill

GISS: The shape and size of a jalapeño

RANGE: The western US, southern Canada, Gulf Coast, and Mexico

DID YOU KNOW . . .

Hummingbirds have the fastest wingbeat of all birds. It varies from species to species but rufous hummingbirds have been clocked flapping 52 to 62 times per second. This hummingbird species pushes further north during breeding season than any other, reaching the 61st parallel in Alaska. If you measure according to body length, at just over 3 inches they have the longest migration of any other bird species. Flower nectar is a big part of their diet, but they also eat tiny insects including aphids and midges.

YELLOW WARBLER *(yell-oh war-blur)*

Small and vocal, these birds are common in wetlands and tend to nest low to the ground. Males are bright yellow with scarlet streaking down the front. Females are a paler version of the males. Cowbirds frequently leave eggs in this insectivore's nest, so you will sometimes see these small yellow birds feeding a brown bird twice their size.

COLOR: Yellow

HEAD: Dark eye, small bill

GISS: The shape and size of a Ping-Pong ball

RANGE: Widespread in North America

FEMALE

MALE

BALTIMORE ORIOLE
(BALL-teh-more OR-ee-ole)

Males are bright orange with black wings and white wing bars. Females vary between orange and yellow with buff to gray backs. Orioles prefer wooded edges or open woods, especially near water. Largely insectivores, they will also feed on fruit, nectar, and grape jelly. They weave pendulous nests on the ends of branches to raise their young. Females resemble males as they age.

COLOR: Orange and black, some yellow

HEAD: Round with a long, pointed beak

GISS: The shape of a submarine and the size of a tennis ball

RANGE: The eastern US and southern Canada

FEMALE

MALE

BULLOCK'S ORIOLE *(bull-awks OR-ee-ole)*

Males are blaze orange with black on the top of the head and back, and a black eyeline. Their wings are black with bold patches of white, and the tail is black with orange edging. Females have dull yellow heads and tails with grayish backs and wings and white wing bars, and their bellies are off-white. Bullock's orioles will breed with Baltimore orioles where their ranges overlap. They like tall, mature trees that are spaced out rather than heavily wooded areas.

COLOR: Orange, black, white, gray, and yellow

HEAD: Round with a pointed gray beak

GISS: The shape of a submarine and the size of a tennis ball

RANGE: The western US

MALE

FEMALE

BLACK-CHINNED HUMMINGBIRD
(blak-CHIN-ed hum-ing-bird)

Black-chinned hummingbirds are green on the back with white bellies. Males have a black throat, with a narrow band of iridescent purple under their black bibs. Females lack the black chin (bib) entirely and have white tips to their outer feathers. They like open woods and, in the Southwest, they are the hummingbird you'll find along rivers in canyons. Most of the sounds you hear from hummingbirds are made from the rapid beating of their wings. All hummingbirds give a sputtery squeaky chirp when chasing, and a displaying male makes a buzzy trill.

COLOR: Green and white, black chin

HEAD: Small, with a long, thin bill

GISS: The shape and size of a jalapeño

RANGE: The western US and Mexico

MALE

FEMALE

RUBY-THROATED HUMMINGBIRD
(ROO-bee throw-ted hum-ing-bird)

This feisty green meanie of a hummingbird is found in yards full of nectar-rich plants and small insects. Males flash a red chin, which can look black in the shade. Females lack the ruby throat and can be distinguished from males because of the white tips on the tail feathers. Females only use males for copulation and raise the young on their own. Ruby-throats can cross the Gulf of Mexico on their own two wings during migration. These birds can be aggressive with one another.

COLOR: Green

HEAD: Menacing-looking, with a long, thin beak

GISS: The shape and size of a jalapeño

RANGE: Eastern US into southern Canada

FEMALE

MALE

FOUR SONGBIRDS (PARK BIRDS)

This is a huge bronze-y-green bird with a bare head, pale blue skin, and a red chin. Its body has distinct brown and white flight feathers. The tail is also bronze and striped with pale edges. Males sport a ropelike beard off the chest. As gangly and strange as these birds are, they are adept at navigating urban environments, can feed out of almost any seed feeder, and roost high in trees at night.

COLOR: Bronze, green, red, and light blue

HEAD: Bare, with knobby skin, a red chin, and a pale beak

GISS: The shape and size of a beach ball

RANGE: The US

DID YOU KNOW . . .

Turkeys spend most of their waking hours foraging on the ground and eat anything from seeds and fruit to insects and amphibians. Most of their movement is on foot, but they can fly up into trees where they roost or sleep at night, although hens nest on the ground. The wild turkey was in steep decline in the 20th century due to hunting and habitat loss. Hundreds of thousands of turkeys were subsequently reintroduced to the lower 48 states. Now the population is back to the levels of pre-European settlement and they are fast becoming an urban bird in many communities.

EASTERN TOWHEE *(ease-tern tow-hee)*

Males are strikingly black and white with reddish-brown sides. Females resemble males but are brown and white with rusty sides. Some birds show a few spots on the back. Towhees make a variety of sounds alerting you to their presence. Males sing atop small trees and shrubs and sound like they are shouting, "DRINK your teaaaa!" or give a "twee" contact call. They look very similar to the spotted towhee and will even hybridize.

COLOR: Black, white, and reddish-brown

HEAD: Round with a conical beak

GISS: The shape and size of a tennis ball, with a tail

RANGE: The eastern US

FEMALE

MALE

ROSE-BREASTED GROSBEAK
(rose-brest-id gross-beek)

Rose-breasted grosbeak males are black on their backs and heads, with white bellies. They have a rosy-pink triangle on their breast and a thick, conical beak like a cardinal. Females are streaky brown and white, with a bold white eyebrow; they resemble giant female purple finches. Young males resemble females with hints of salmon on the chest. These plump birds will show up to feeders during migration, especially those with sunflower or safflower.

COLOR: Black, white, brown, and pink

HEAD: Round with a large, thick beak, white eyebrow in females

GISS: Plump, the shape and size of a tennis ball

RANGE: Eastern and central North America

MALE

FEMALE

SPOTTED TOWHEE *(spot-TED tow-hee)*

Males are strikingly black and white with rufous (reddish-brown) sides. Females resemble males but are brown and white with rusty sides. Birds are heavily spotted on the back. Males sing atop small trees and shrubs and sound like they are shouting. Although they look similar to the eastern towhee, they don't have the catchphrase. Instead, they trill quite a bit, and their call is a raspy "caaaaaaw."

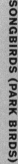

COLOR: Black, white, and reddish-brown

HEAD: Round with a conical beak

GISS: The shape and size of a tennis ball, with a tail

RANGE: The western US

SONGBIRDS (PARK BIRDS)

BLACK-BILLED MAGPIE *(bla-k bill-ed mag-pi)*

This black-and-white bird with a tail that is as long as its body is hard to miss. In the sun, these birds show a greenish-blue iridescence on the wings. In California, you might see the yellow-billed magpie, which looks almost identical apart from its yellow bill. Magpies build giant, ball-like nests that can take over a month to put together.

COLOR: Black and white

HEAD: Round with a pointed bill

GISS: The shape and size of a softball, with a long tail

RANGE: Central and northwestern North America

BROWN THRASHER *(broun THRash-her)*

Living up to its name, you can find this brown-plumaged bird in your yard tossing leaves while looking for food. Thrashers are brown on the back and head and sport a long tail. Their undersides are white with black streaks. These birds are mimics like mockingbirds and will sing the songs of other birds, usually repeating each phrase twice. They like very thick bushes on the edge of wooded areas.

COLOR: Brown, white, and black

HEAD: Oval, with a long beak that curves slightly downward

GISS: The shape and size of a softball, with a long tail

RANGE: Eastern and central US

CHIPPING SPARROW *(chip-ping spare-oh)*

The trill of this summer sparrow is a constant in many yards and cemeteries. Chipping sparrows are distinctive looking with their rusty red caps, white eyebrow, and a black line through the eye. They look similar to American tree sparrows but lack the central breast spot. Chipping sparrows molt into a duller plumage for the winter and can trick some people during fall migration.

COLOR: Rust, gray, black, and white

HEAD: White eyebrow, black eye line, short dark beak

GISS: The shape and size of a Ping-Pong ball, with a tail

RANGE: Widespread in North America

AMERICAN TREE SPARROW
(Ah-mer-i-can tr-EE spare-oh)

This sparrow typically shows up in winter and, with its rusty cap, can easily be mistaken for the chipping sparrow. But this bird's bicolored (dark on top and yellow on the bottom) bill as well as its central breast spot give it away. Typically found feeding in grassy areas, they will show up to bird feeders and forage on the ground for white millet or sunflower chips.

COLOR: Gray, rust, and white

HEAD: Round and striped, with a conical beak

GISS: The shape and size of a Ping-Pong ball

RANGE: North America

SONGBIRDS (PARK BIRDS)

SONG SPARROW *(song spare-oh)*

This common striped sparrow is typically found near water, nesting in thick cover. Song sparrows have a gray face and back with a white breast. These birds are covered in thick stripes all over, with

a spot forming on the central breast. Their color varies by region, with birds in the east being redder and birds in the west being grayer. They sing constantly once on territory and are highly responsive to pishing.

COLOR: Gray, white, and brown

HEAD: Striped, with a thick, conical beak

GISS: The shape and size of a Ping-Pong ball, with a long tail

RANGE: Widespread in North America

BEWICK'S WREN *(Boo-wix ren)*

This wren is brown with a long gray tail that is flicking when it's not cocked up in the air. Bewick's wrens have a bold white eyebrow and white chin and breast. In areas where they share space with house wrens, their nests are vulnerable to takeover by the house wrens, which will remove the Bewick eggs and nestlings to take over the nests.

COLOR: Brown, with a gray tail and white chin and breast

HEAD: Flat, bold eyebrow, and a thin, curved beak

GISS: The shape and size of a Ping-Pong ball, with a flicking tail

RANGE: The west and southwest US

BUSHTIT *(bush-tit)*

These small gray birds have a long tail and live in flocks with dozens of birds. Bushtits have brownish heads and females have a bold pale eye compared to males, who have a black eye. Bushtits will converge and cover a suet feeder as a flock. During breeding season, other bushtits, apart from the breeding pair, will assist with care of the young.

COLOR: Gray and brown

HEAD: Round with a compact beak

GISS: The shape and size of a dust bunny, with a long tail

RANGE: The western US

EASTERN KINGBIRD *(ease-turn king-burd)*

Eastern kingbirds have a white belly and neck and a black head and back. Tails are black with a distinctive white stripe on the tail tip. Occasionally, during breeding season, they will reveal an orange patch on the top of the head. They usually perch prominently on the tops of trees calling and flying out to catch passing insects.

COLOR: Black and white

HEAD: Round, rough feathers on top, flat, pointy beak, orange patch on top

GISS: The shape of a submarine and the size of a tennis ball

RANGE: Central and eastern US and Canada

SONGBIRDS (PARK BIRDS)

WESTERN KINGBIRD *(wes-turn king-burd)*

Western kingbirds perch on power lines and are noticeable for their gray backs, yellow bellies, and white cheeks. When agitated, they will reveal a red patch on the very tops of their heads. Western kingbirds have been expanding their range east and are beginning to overlap with eastern kingbirds in some areas. They can be very aggressive around nesting territory.

COLOR: Gray, yellow, and white

HEAD: Flat black beak, red patch on top

GISS: The shape of a submarine and the size of a tennis ball

RANGE: The western US

GREATER ROADRUNNER *(grate-er rode-ruhn-er)*

This scraggly brownish bird doesn't look anything like its cartoon counterpart. Roadrunners are streaky brown and white, with a long, dark tail, and a scraggly bunch of dark feathers and a bold light eyebrow on the head. Males will flash red behind the eye. They generally trot along the ground but will use their wings to flap up into cover. These carnivores eat rodents and lizards and have been known to stake out bird feeders to grab unsuspecting sparrows and hummingbirds.

COLOR: Dark brown and white

HEAD: Scruffy with a bold eye stripe and long, thin bill

GISS: Like a stretched-out chicken, the size of a volleyball

RANGE: The southwestern US

BLUE-GRAY GNATCATCHER
(blew-gr-ay nat-cat-cher)

Heard more than seen, the gnatcatcher repeatedly makes a high-pitched, nasally thin call. Adults are light gray on back and even lighter gray on the belly. Their tails are long and black with white feathers on either side. Their faces show a distinct white eye-ring, and during breeding season, males develop a prominent black unibrow.

COLOR: Gray with black and white tail

HEAD: Eye-ring, occasional unibrow

GISS: The shape and size of a Ping-Pong ball, with a long, upright tail

RANGE: The US

CLIFF SWALLOW *(kliff swah-low)*

Cliff swallows are rarely found alone and are usually spotted in a large flock of birds circling around a bridge. With a dark navy-blue back, a dark rusty face, a small black bill, and a pale unibrow, this bird resembles a barn swallow. It just lacks the deeply forked tail and has a squared-off tail. They nest in colonies under bridges and eaves, making cavity structures of mud and their saliva.

COLOR: Navy and rust

HEAD: Unibrow, short black beak

GISS: The shape and size of a paper airplane

RANGE: Widespread in North America

SONGBIRDS (PARK BIRDS)

BROWN CREEPER *(brow-nn kree-purr)*

Resembling a small piece of bark hitching up the trunk of a tree, this bird can be easily overlooked. Brown creepers are brown and mottled white and buff on the back. The breast is white, and they have a long stiff tail. They use their thin, curved beak to look for insects and spiders in bark. During migration, they can be found in

loose flocks with kinglets in any place that has mature trees.

COLOR: Brown, white, and buff

HEAD: Small, with a thin, curved beak

GISS: The shape of a piece of bark and the size of a bar of soap from a hotel

RANGE: The US

INDIGO BUNTING
(in-dig-go bun-ting)

Males are dark blue, appearing almost black in the shade, and females are brown with no other markings. These birds are quite common and, being sparrow-sized, easy to miss. They typically prefer a wooded edge near a field with a lake, pond, or creek nearby. Indigo buntings will show up to bird feeders during migration if insects are scarce. Males sing all day at the tops of trees during breeding season, even in the heat of July.

COLOR: Blue or brown

HEAD: Scruffy with a dainty, conical beak

GISS: The shape and size of a Ping-Pong ball

RANGE: The eastern US

FEMALE

MALE

PILEATED WOODPECKER
(pie-lee-ate-ted wood-peck-her or
PILL-ee-ate-ted wood-peck-her)

There is disagreement over how this bird's name is pronounced. This crow-sized black woodpecker sports a red crest (to which the "pileated" of its name refers) and white wing patches. Males have red extending from their beak to over the head and a red mustache. Females only have red on the back half of the crest. These woodpeckers make distinctive, oval holes in trees and can be found foraging on the ground or on the lower parts of tree trunks looking for insects.

COLOR: Black, white, and red

HEAD: Crested, huge beak, red mustache

GISS: The shape and size of a football

RANGE: The eastern US and southern Canada

MALE   FEMALE

YELLOW-BELLIED SAPSUCKER
(yell-oh-bell-eed sap-suck-her)

Yellow-bellied sapsuckers are known as much for the wells that they drill into trees as they are for their field marks. They drill for sap in the spring and for insects in the summer. Males are black and white with a red patch on the forehead and a red chin. Females resemble males but have a white throat patch. Sapsuckers use drumming to announce their territory, and have the rhythm of a Ping-Pong ball bouncing when they peck.

COLOR: Black, white, and red

HEAD: Red forehead patch with a long black beak

GISS: The shape and size of an ice-cream cone

RANGE: The eastern US and Canada

NORTHERN BOBWHITE *(nor-thurn bob-whyte)*

Bobwhites are known for their two-note song that sounds like they are singing, "Bob white." Most bobwhites are mottled brown, black, and white with a white patch on the face and a short, curved beak. The colors can vary between habitats because the colors of the habitats themselves vary.

COLOR: Brown, white, and black

HEAD: Scruffy with a cheek patch and short, curved beak

GISS: The shape and size of a softball

RANGE: The southeastern US

PURPLE MARTIN *(purr-pull mar-tan)*

A large, noisy swallow, males look almost black in the shade and are a dark purple in the sun. Females are purple on the back, wings, and head, with a gray breast. These colony-nesting insectivores will use birdhouses or gourds to nest in, but they are very picky about the location. They prefer houses that are the highest thing within a 150-foot diameter and next to open water.

COLOR: Dark purple and gray

HEAD: Round with a short, flat beak

GISS: The shape and size of a paper airplane

RANGE: The eastern US and parts of western California

MALE

FEMALE

BREWER'S BLACKBIRD
(Bru-ers blak-burd)

This western blackbird is easy to confuse with the grackle, but its diminutive size gives it away. Males in breeding plumage are iridescent purple and green with a bold yellow eye and short tail (when compared to grackles). Females are brown with darker wings and tail. Sometimes their eyes are dark. In winter, males molt into a drabber plumage and their heads and chests resemble females. They tend to like open areas, yards, parks, farms, and woods near water.

COLOR: Glossy green and purple, brown

HEAD: Round, with a bright iris and a conical bill

GISS: Sleek, the shape and size of a tennis ball

RANGE: Western and central US and Canada

MALE

FEMALE

CASSIN'S FINCH *(Kass-ins fin-ch)*

Typically found in mountainous regions in the west, this finch is an accomplished singer that can mimic the calls of other birds. Males are rosy pink and usually have a brighter cap. Females are white with brown streaking all over the body and a distinct brown cheek patch. These birds tend to nest in loose colonies and are not the finches you find in your hanging plant baskets.

COLOR: White, brown, and pink

HEAD: Rough, thick, conical beak; female cheek patch

GISS: The shape and size of a Ping-Pong ball

RANGE: The western US

FEMALE

MALE

CLARK'S NUTCRACKER *(Klar-Ks nut-crak-er)*

Large, bold, and sassy, this member of the crow and jay family is a big fan of pine seeds. Nutcrackers are medium-sized birds that are pale gray overall with black wings and white patches on the tail. They are known for using their specialized bills to get seeds out of pine cones and for their ability to cache thousands of seeds and remember their locations for eating later. You'll most likely find them in coniferous woods at high elevations.

COLOR: Gray, black, and white

HEAD: Round with a long, thin, pointy beak

GISS: The shape of a submarine and the size of a volleyball

RANGE: Mountains of western US

FOX SPARROW *(fahks spare-oh)*

This large sparrow will catch your attention in your yard when you witness it kicking leaves out of its way when it feeds. The birds vary in plumage color but are generally reddish-brown on the wings and tail with a gray back and face; they're also heavily spotted on the chest with a prominent central breast spot and pale bill. In the west, birds tend to show more gray than reddish-brown. When they migrate, they often mix in with white-throated sparrows.

COLOR: Rust and gray

HEAD: Round with a conical, pale bill

GISS: Robust, the shape and size of a Ping-Pong ball, with a tail

RANGE: Widespread in North America

GREAT CRESTED FLYCATCHER
(grate kress-ted fly-cat-chur)

This medium-sized bird is heard far more often than seen as it screams, "Reep reep reep," from the tops of trees. When the bird flies low, you can detect its lovely yellow undersides, accented by its gray head and rusty red wings and tails. Great crested flycatchers are cavity nesters and will sometimes take over larger bluebird boxes or wood duck boxes. They usually leave a snakeskin in the nest.

COLOR: Yellow, rust, and gray

HEAD: Shaggy with a thin beak

GISS: The shape of a submarine and the size of a tennis ball

RANGE: The eastern US

SONGBIRDS (PARK BIRDS)

SWAINSON'S THRUSH *(Swane-sons thr-uh-sh)*

Gray-and-buff versions of a hermit thrush, Swainson's thrushes have a rising song and can also harmonize with themselves. Gray on the head, back, wings, and tail, they have a white breast with gray spots and a yellowish-buff wash over the face and chest. Swainson's thrushes will sometimes incorporate fungus into their nests, which may help to deter nest parasites.

COLOR: Buff, gray, and white

HEAD: Eye-ring with a thin beak

GISS: The shape and size of a tennis ball

RANGE: Widespread in the US

This unassuming bird has a rusty back and tail, brown back and head, and white breast with black spots. Hermit thrushes have haunting songs that can produce two notes at once, allowing the bird to harmonize with itself. During migration, they will forage the leaf litter in woods, quietly flipping leaves looking for invertebrates.

COLOR: Brown, rust, and white

HEAD: Round with a thin bill

GISS: The shape and size of a tennis ball

RANGE: Widespread in North America

DID YOU KNOW . . .

The haunting song of the hermit thrush may sound beautiful and relaxing to humans, but to males of the species they are a battle cry to defend their territory. Hermit thrushes nest differently based on region. In the eastern part of North America, they nest on the ground; in the West, they nest in trees. Females build the nest out of a variety of plant fibers including moss, bark strips, ferns, and rootlets. Though primarily insect eaters, hermit thrushes also eat fruit, and you can find them feeding on grapes, mistletoe berries, elderberries, serviceberries, and pokeberries.

HORNED LARK *(hor-ned lar-kk)*

These gray-brown birds have a black mask, black collar, and thin black horns on the tops of their heads. They are most often seen as you travel down a gravel road around farm fields, and they fly away revealing black tail feathers. Horned larks will hover in the air over their breeding territory, making a tinkling, bell-like call. Recently, a bird found in melting permafrost turned out to be a 46,000-year-old horned lark.

COLOR: Gray, brown, and black

HEAD: Black mask and horns

GISS: Upright, the shape and size of a Ping-Pong ball, with a tail and horns

RANGE: Widespread in North America

LOGGERHEAD SHRIKE
(log-er-hed SHRykk)

There are two species of shrike in the US that look almost identical. The most common is the loggerhead shrike, which looks like a chickadee on steroids. They are dark gray on the back with a black mask, black wings, a tail with patches of white, and a white chin and chest. They are known for catching insects, mice, small birds, and lizards and impaling them on barbs of fences or bushes.

COLOR: Gray, black, and white

HEAD: Masked with a medium beak with slight hook at the tip

GISS: The shape and size of a tennis ball, with a tail

RANGE: The US

ORANGE-CROWNED WARBLER
(or-range cround war-blur)

The dullest, most nondescript warbler out there, this bird stands out for its lack of field marks. If you notice an olive-colored warbler with maybe the hint of an eyebrow and no interesting behavior, chances are good it's an orange-crowned. The orange is rarely visible unless you are holding the bird in your hand. They breed in dense wooded areas but during migration can be found anywhere.

COLOR: Olive and orange (if you're lucky)

HEAD: Round with a faint eyeline (line that goes through where their eye is on their head), thin beak

GISS: The shape and size of a Ping-Pong ball

RANGE: Widespread in North America

MALE

FEMALE

RING-NECKED PHEASANT *(reeng-nekt Fez-int)*

Introduced from Asia into North America for hunting purposes, pheasants have adapted well to the farming landscapes here. Pheasants are large birds with long, pointed tails. Males tend to be dark rusty on the chest, with a white collar, green head, and red skin around the face. Females are overall buffy with mottled brown and gray on the back and wings.

COLOR: Rust, green, white, buff, and gray

HEAD: Red waddle with a short beak

GISS: The shape and size of a football, with a pointy tail

RANGE: The northern and central US

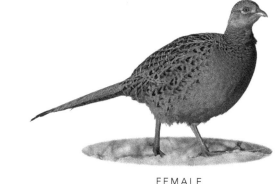

FEMALE

MALE

RUBY-CROWNED KINGLET
(roo-bee-cround king-lett)

This bird is a drab olive color and tends to mix in with warblers during migration. They have dark wings with hints of yellow-and-white wing bars. Their red crown is usually hidden except when participating in aggressive interactions. Ruby-crowns have a long, meandering song that is surprisingly loud for their tiny size. They are highly responsive to pishing. During breeding season, they tend to congregate in dense forests.

COLOR: Olive

HEAD: Small, with a red crown (usually hidden), big eyes, tiny bill

GISS: The shape and size of a dust bunny

RANGE: Widespread in North America

GOLDEN-CROWNED KINGLET
(goal-den-cround king-lett)

These small gray birds have wing bands, a dark eyeline, and a yellow patch on the head that can be raised to show golden orange. Typically, they feed in conifers during migration and nest in boreal forests. Despite their small size, they can tolerate weather well below zero degrees Fahrenheit.

COLOR: Gray

HEAD: Tiny, with a frustrated look and a yellow patch

GISS: The shape and size of a Ping-Pong ball

RANGE: Widespread in North America

SAY'S PHOEBE *(Sayz fee-bee)*

A medium-sized dark bird of the West, Say's phoebes are gray on the back and tail with a darker gray head and a salmon wash over the belly and vent. These insectivores will use yards for nesting but will not come to bird feeders. Like many phoebes, they will use the same nest site several years in a row.

COLOR: Gray and salmon

HEAD: Round with a flat, thin beak

GISS: The shape and size of a tennis ball, with a tail

RANGE: Western North America

SONGBIRDS (PARK BIRDS)

MEADOWLARK *(MED-o-lark)*

The eastern and the western species of meadowlarks look very similar: buff, gray, and brown streaks on the back, a short tail, a yellow chest and chin, and a black V across the breast. When they fly, the tail flashes bold white on either side. Most birders can only tell them apart by song. Eastern meadowlarks give a thin whistle resembling "spring of the year." Western meadowlarks have a bold warbling song that sounds like they are saying, "Please pass the

bottle around." They tend to like open such as prairies, grasslands, scrub, and farmlands.

COLOR: Buff, brown, gray, yellow, and black

HEAD: Flat with a long, thin bill

GISS: The shape and size of a softball, with a short tail

RANGE: Widespread in North America

Male scarlet tanagers are a vivid red with black wings and tail. Females are yellow with black wings and tail. It's amazing that something so bright can hide so easily in the tops of oak trees. You can tell when one of these birds is around, though, because it gives a contact call that sounds like "chick burr" over and over. Mainly insectivores, they will eat suet and fruit when there is an unexpected cold snap during migration.

COLOR: Red, black, and yellow

HEAD: Round, with a light beak

GISS: The shape and size of a fat cigar, with a tail

RANGE: The eastern US

FEMALE

MALE

SUMMER TANAGER *(sum-her tan-aig-er)*

Male summer tanagers are red, with a long pale beak. They lack the crest of a cardinal. Females are yellow with olive wings and a long pale bill. Young males look like a mash-up of a male and female; they are yellow with splotches of red on the head, chest, and back.

COLOR: Red and yellow

HEAD: Flat with a long pale beak

GISS: The shape and size of a fat cigar, with a tail

RANGE: The southern US

FEMALE

MALE

WESTERN TANAGER *(wes-turn tan-aig-er)*

Male western tanagers are bright yellow with a bright red head and black wings with white wing bars. Females are yellow with black on the back, black wings, and white wing bars. Some can have a bit of red around their beaks. Like many tanagers, they are drawn to fruit-bearing trees, especially cherries.

COLOR: Yellow, red, and black

HEAD: Flat with a short beak

GISS: The shape and size of a fat cigar, with a tail

RANGE: The western US and southern Canada

MALE

FEMALE

SNOW BUNTING *(sno bun-ting)*

These birds nest in the Arctic in lemming holes or birdhouses, then head down to the northern US in the winter. Most people spot them in the winter when driving through open areas or farmland. You'll notice large flocks of white-and-beige birds flying on the sides of the roads. In winter, males are white with black wingtips and a tan cheek patch. Females are white with patches of brown on the chest and face and mottled brown and black on the back. Both have tiny orange beaks.

COLOR: White, black, and tan

HEAD: Cheek patches with a tiny orange beak

GISS: The shape and size of a Ping-Pong ball

RANGE: Widespread in North America

DID YOU KNOW . . .

Snow buntings make their way to the lower 48 states from Arctic climes in the winter. Most people recognize them as the whitish birds that fly away from the sides of country roads when a car goes by. On their breeding grounds in the Arctic, snow buntings nest in cavities in either crevices or old lemming holes. In towns in the Arctic, snow buntings will even use homemade birdhouses.

YELLOW-HEADED BLACKBIRD
(yell-oh-hed-id blak-bird)

Males are black with a bright yellow head, and white wing patches; they are unmistakable. Females are brownish black with pale yellow on the face and chest. They probably have the most unharmonious song of any bird in North America, like a loud screeching bullfrog that drowns out the songs of other birds in the marsh or farm field.

COLOR: Black, yellow, and white

HEAD: Round with a conical beak

GISS: Roughly the shape and size of a tennis ball

RANGE: The western and central US and Canada

MALE

FEMALE

BOBOLINK *(bob-o-link)*

These birds are noted for their complex songs, which ring across fields and prairies. Males are black, with a bleached-blond-looking cap and white patches on the wings and rump. Females are buff with brown stripes on the back and flanks and a black cap. After breeding season, male bobolinks molt new feathers and look like the females. These ground-nesting birds spend winters in South America.

COLOR: Black, white, brown, and buff

HEAD: Round, with a thick, conical bill

GISS: The shape of a submarine and the size of a tennis ball

RANGE: Eastern and central US and Canada

MALE

FEMALE

FIVE SHOREBIRDS AND WATERBIRDS

MALLARD *(mal-ard)*

This is the most common duck you will find in the US. Males have a shiny green head, bright yellow bill, gray body, brown chest, bright orange feet, and white tail with black curly feathers. Females are mottled dark brown and buff with a prominent eye-ring and cap. Their beaks are black and orange. After the females mate with the males, they will incubate the eggs and raise the ducklings alone. They live in fresh water.

COLOR: Green, buff, brown, and gray

HEAD: Round with a rounded flat beak

GISS: Classic duck shape

RANGE: Widespread in North America

FEMALE

MALE

SWAN *(Sw-ahn)*

There are three swan species in North America; all are large and white with subtle differences to the face. Trumpeter swans and tundra swans both have black beaks, but tundra swans have a yellow spot on the base of their bill. Both are quite vocal, with trumpeters sounding like toy horns and tundra swans sounding like yippy dogs. Mute swans have been newly introduced to North America. As a result, the ecosystem is not used to them, they do a lot of damage to fish breeding habitats, and they kill nesting ducks and geese. Their honking sounds like flatulence.

COLOR: White

HEAD: Small, round with a dark beak

GISS: The shape and size of a beach ball, with a long, lanky neck attached

RANGE: Water in North America

DID YOU KNOW . . .

Tundra swans nest in the Arctic but can be found in large flocks migrating over the United States in early spring and late fall. They spend the winter in the Chesapeake Bay on the East Coast. Trumpeter swans were endangered in the 20th century but reintroduction programs in the lower 48 states have made them a common breeding bird in the upper Midwest and parts of the western United States with open water.

SHOREBIRDS AND WATERBIRDS

CANADA GOOSE *(Can-a-da goo-se)*

The bane of joggers and bike riders, Canada geese are widespread and highly adaptable. With their fat brown bodies, long black necks, and jaunty white chin straps, these geese are easy to identify. They vary in size, but if you see one about the size of a mallard, it could be a cackling goose. Birders are more likely to refer to these birds as "cobra chicken" because they hiss and have long necks.

COLOR: Brown, white, and black

HEAD: Small with a rounded beak

GISS: The shape and size of a beach ball, with a cobra-like neck

RANGE: Everywhere. They could be inside your house right now.

HERRING GULL *(hair-ring guhl)*

Adult herring gulls are white with a light gray back and wings, with black-and-white tips. They have pink legs and a yellow bill with a red spot. In winter, these gulls will show gray on the head and neck. Immature birds are mottled dark brown, gray, and white with pink bills with a dark tip. You'll find them around water and city dumps.

COLOR: White, gray, and pink

HEAD: Chunky, round head and a yellow beak with a red spot

GISS: Large, hefty bird, like the shape of a duck but with bouncy wings

RANGE: Widespread in the US

RING-BILLED GULL *(ring-bill-ed guhl)*

Adults are white with pale gray wings that have black-and-white feather tips. In winter, the adults will have gray streaking on the back of the neck. They have a yellow bill with a black ring and yellow feet. Immature birds are mottled gray and brown with a black beak. Gull species in the US are notoriously hard to identify because they go through so many molts and look similar to other types of gulls. Very few birders are experts at figuring them out.

COLOR: Gray, white, black, and yellow

HEAD: Round with a short, stubby beak

GISS: A bouncy baseball shape, with long, tapered wings.

RANGE: Widespread in North America

ADULT

JUVENILE

SHOREBIRDS AND
WATERBIRDS

GREAT BLUE HERON
(gray-t blew hair-ahn)

These huge birds are gray-blue with long necks and a black-and-white crest. Great blue herons can be found anywhere there is open water so they can hunt for fish, small birds, rodents, frogs, snakes, and pretty much anything else their beaks can hold. They nest in large colonies in trees called rookeries.

COLOR: Gray-blue, black, and white

HEAD: Slender and crested, with a long, spear-like beak

GISS: Lanky, about the height of a toddler

RANGE: Widespread in North America

DID YOU KNOW . . .

Great blue herons are not the best parents. In many species of songbirds, if a chick falls out of the nest early, the parents will attempt to raise it. If a great blue heron chick falls from the nest, the parent completely forgets its existence. Young herons are very aggressive with each other, and if adults are not bringing in enough food, larger young will push smaller young out of the nest. Adult herons make guttural squawking sounds that almost make one wonder if that's what dinosaurs sounded like. Be wary at a heron rookery, if you startle the birds they will vomit down as a defense mechanism.

GREAT EGRET *(grate ee-gret)*

This long, lanky white bird has a long, sharp beak. They are smaller than great blue herons but are the largest white herons in the US.

The snowy egret is similar in appearance, but the great egret has black toes. They nest in large colonies called rookeries.

COLOR: White

HEAD: Horizontal with a long yellow beak

GISS: The shape and size of a deflated beach ball

RANGE: The eastern US and coastal states

KILLDEER *(kill-dee-ear)*

This is a noisy bird that can be heard repeating the sound "kill deer" all day and night. Killdeer are brown on the back with white bellies. Heads are brown and white, with two distinct black stripes around the neck and chest. If something gets too close to the nest, the parents will stretch out their wings and tail, revealing reddish orange feathers, which make it look as if the bird is mortally wounded. A wounded bird attracts the attention of predators and diverts them from baby birds.

COLOR: Brown and white

HEAD: Round with a long, flat beak, apologetic-looking face

GISS: The shape and size of a sideways ice-cream cone

RANGE: Widespread in North America

BELTED KINGFISHER *(bell-tid king-fish-her)*

Belted kingfishers show up along lakes, rivers, and streams and make loud, rattle-like calls as they fly along seeking fish, crayfish, and frogs. Kingfishers have big, shaggy crests and a chunky, spear-like beak. Females have dark blue backs, heads, and necklaces, with rufous (reddish-brown) along the flanks and across the belly. Males resemble females but lack the rufous. Watch for them on open branches near water or on power lines. They often hover before they dive.

COLOR: Blue and reddish-brown

HEAD: Large, shaggy crest, dark bill, spear-like beak

GISS: The shape and size of a softball

RANGE: Open water in North America

AMERICAN COOT *(Ah-mer-i-can koot)*

Coots resemble black ducks with short white beaks, but they are more closely related to cranes and rails. When out of the water, coots have long, gangly legs and strange-looking lobed toes (toes that are separated from one another unlike the webbed toes of ducks). A large flock is called a raft of coots. Coots tend to like fresh water with lots of vegetation they can eat.

COLOR: Black and white

HEAD: Small, with a short, bright white beak

GISS: The shape and size of a football

RANGE: Open water in North America

COMMON YELLOWTHROAT
(comm-on yell-oh-throw-t)

These warblers nest low in vegetation near water. They are found in marshes singing nonstop alongside red-winged blackbirds. Typically heard more than seen, their "which-ity which-ity which-ity" call will burn itself in your brain. Males are olive on the tail, back, and head and yellow on the belly, and have a black mask bordered by white. Females lack the black mask, and young birds lack most of the yellow. They are generally very responsive to pishing. When they do come out of hiding, they have a hunched-over appearance that, when combined with the mask, makes them look like they've been up to something suspicious.

COLOR: Olive, yellow, and black

HEAD: Black mask on males, short black beak

GISS: The shape, size, and texture of a dust bunny

RANGE: Widespread in North America

FEMALE

MALE

DOUBLE-CRESTED CORMORANT
(dub-el kress-ted kor-more-rant)

Of the six species of cormorant living in the United States, the double-crested is the most common. These black birds can swim like ducks but have a noticeable thin beak that is hooked at the end, which is helpful in hooking and catching fish. They swim with just their neck and heads sticking out of the water and live anywhere there is water and fish.

COLOR: Black

HEAD: Horizontal, oval head with a thin, hooked beak

GISS: The shape and size of a football, with a gangly neck

RANGE: Coasts of the US and North America

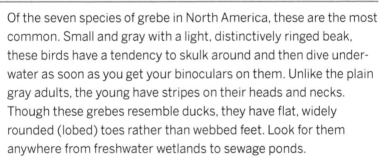

PIED-BILLED GREBE *(pie-d bill-ed greee-b)*

Of the seven species of grebe in North America, these are the most common. Small and gray with a light, distinctively ringed beak, these birds have a tendency to skulk around and then dive underwater as soon as you get your binoculars on them. Unlike the plain gray adults, the young have stripes on their heads and necks. Though these grebes resemble ducks, they have flat, widely rounded (lobed) toes rather than webbed feet. Look for them anywhere from freshwater wetlands to sewage ponds.

COLOR: Light gray

HEAD: Dainty, beak with a dark ring

GISS: Half the size of a football

RANGE: Widespread on open fresh water in the US and Canada

WHITE IBIS *(why-tt i-bis)*

Adults are bright white with pink legs; a long, curved pink bill; and blue eyes. Young birds are brown on back or mottled brown and white with a streaked head and neck. Adapted to wade in shallow

wetlands and use their beaks to probe for invertebrates in the mud, these birds will also congregate in urban areas and beg for food.

COLOR: White and pink

HEAD: Small head, long, curved pink bill shaped like a sickle

GISS: The shape and size of a football, with a long neck

RANGE: Gulf Coast states

WHITE-FACED IBIS *(why-t fay-st i-biz)*

This lanky bird is iridescent brown with green wings. The adult face has pink bordered by white and a long, curved bill. A bird like this along the Gulf, lacking the pink, could be the similar glossy ibis. Spot them most frequently in flooded fields, wetlands, and marshes.

COLOR: Iridescent brown, green, pink, and white

HEAD: Small with a long, dark, downward-curving bill shaped like a sickle

GISS: The shape and size of a football, with a long neck

RANGE: The central and western United States

This lanky, aquatic bird swims with just its head and neck above water, earning it the nickname "snake bird." Males are black with white wing patches, white streaks down the back, and a long tail with a buff edge. Females have a buff head, neck, and chest. The anhinga, like a hawk, can soar in warm currents of air that spiral upward. After swimming for fish, they will perch in trees and extend their wings to dry out their feathers.

COLOR: Black, white, and buff

HEAD: Small with a long, sharp yellow beak

GISS: The shape of a football and the size of a beach ball, with a snakelike neck

RANGE: Gulf Coast states

FEMALE

MALE

LEAST SANDPIPER *(lee-st san-d-pie-per)*

In a world where small sandpipers tend to look alike, these are easy to identify. If it's extra tiny and the bill is a different color than the legs, it's a least sandpiper. Sparrow-sized with a long, tapered dark bill, it's rusty brown on the back, head, and chest with a white belly. The legs are lighter colored than the bill, even when covered with mud. They will be the smallest shorebird running around in the flock.

COLOR: Rusty brown and white

HEAD: Long, tapered black bill

GISS: The shape and size of a pinball, on sticks

RANGE: Widespread in North America

SPOTTED SANDPIPER *(spot-ted sand-pie-per)*

Found along lakes, wetlands, and rivers, this small, fast shorebird has a habit of bobbing its tail up and down, which is a more reliable identification feature than its spots. After all, the spots disappear in winter, so for half the year, the spotted sandpiper has no spots. A spotted sandpiper is gray on the back and white on the belly, with spots in the summer. It flies low over the water with shallow wingbeats and gives off peep notes.

COLOR: Gray and white

HEAD: Eyebrow with a long, thin, orange beak

GISS: The shape and size of a Ping-Pong ball, with toothpick-like legs

RANGE: Widespread in North America

SANDERLING *(san-der-ling)*

When breeding, sanderlings have a plumage that is mottled rusty brown, black on the head, back, and chest, and white on the belly. When not breeding, their plumage is silvery gray with a dark mark on the shoulder. Sanderlings quickly run back and forth with the waves as they feed on the coast. In wetlands, they are a bit more chill. They only have three toes, unlike most birds, which have four.

COLOR: Brown, silvery, and white

HEAD: Round, black bill

GISS: The shape and size of a tennis ball, on sticks

RANGE: Coasts of North America and central US

WILLET *(will-it)*

The willet is a medium-sized, mottled gray shorebird with a long-tapered beak. The bird shows mostly gray until in flight, when the wing feathers flash patches of black with a bold white stripe. Usually, one or two willets will be mixed in with a flock of other smaller shorebirds. They are common on beaches and in wetlands.

COLOR: Gray

HEAD: Round with a long, tapered beak

GISS: The shape and size of a softball, with gangly legs and neck

RANGE: Coasts of US and in the west central US

WOOD DUCK *(wuh-d duh-ck)*

This is a dainty and classy-looking duck. Males have a green head with a bit of white striping and a mullet shape to the back of the head. The body is rusty brown and buff with a dark back. Females have a shaggy crest, white eye-ring, dark beak, and brown body, with a blue patch on the wing. Wood ducks nest in tree cavities or wood duck nesting boxes, and the young can fall 50 feet (safely) after hatching.

COLOR: Green and brown

HEAD: Mullet-shaped, dainty beak

GISS: Elegant-looking, the shape and size of a football

RANGE: Open fresh water in the US

MALE

FEMALE

GREEN HERON *(green HAIR-ahn)*

This small heron perches low to the shore on dead tree branches. It has a green body with a reddish-brown neck, a dark cap, and a long dark beak. Green herons usually have a hunched-over-looking posture but will occasionally extend their necks. They will drop anything from dried leaves to dog food into the water to draw fish to them.

COLOR: Dark green and reddish-brown, with brown, white, and black streaks

HEAD: Flat, with a fishing spear–like beak with yellow accents

GISS: Hunched over, lanky build, the size of a football

RANGE: Coasts of North America and the eastern US

SANDHILL CRANE *(sand-hill cray-ne)*

These large birds are gray but sometimes stain their feathers with mud during breeding season, giving them a rusty or brown look. They tend to form giant flocks in migration and fly with their necks extended.

COLOR: Gray and rusty-looking

HEAD: Small and round with a red skin patch and long bill

GISS: The shape and size of a basketball, with a long neck and long legs

RANGE: Widespread in western and central North America and in Florida

HOODED MERGANSER *(hood-ed mer-gans-zer)*

The males of this breed of duck are an exquisite black with rusty flanks. During breeding season, they extend their crests, giving the appearance of a perfectly round black head with a bold white patch. They have a thin, hooked black beak. Females are brown and gray, with a scraggly crest. Both have yellow eyes. Sometimes mergansers will use wood duck boxes for nesting.

COLOR: Black, white, rust, gray, and brown

HEAD: Round (male) or scraggly (female) with a thin, hooked beak

GISS: Elegant, the shape and size of a volleyball

RANGE: Widespread in most of the US

FEMALE

MALE

BLACK-NECKED STILT *(blak-neked still-t)*

A slim and elegant bird with long, toothpick-like pink legs that explain the name. Stilts are white with black wings and back and black on their heads. They have a long, pencil-thin black beak and are some of the noisiest birds in the wetlands.

COLOR: Black, white, and pink

HEAD: Round with a pencil-thin black beak

GISS: Origami-like, the shape and size of an emaciated tennis ball, with long legs and neck

RANGE: Coasts of North America and in the western US

AMERICAN AVOCET *(Ah-mer-i-can ahv-oh-set)*

This elegant black-and-white bird has a needlelike bill that curves upward. During the breeding season, adults get a peach wash to the head and neck. In the winter, the peach turns to light gray. Males have straighter bills than females. These birds seek out shallow water, whether it's fresh, salt, or sewage.

COLOR: Black and white

HEAD: Small, with a long, thin, upturned bill

GISS: The shape and size of a softball, with long legs, neck, and beak

RANGE: Coasts of the western US and wetlands in southern Canada

WILSON'S PHALAROPE *(Will-sons fal-a-rohpe)*

Females are white birds with a gray back with rusty-brown patches on the wings, a black stripe that goes from the eyes down the neck and over the back, and rust on the neck. Males are duller than the females in this species, with a pale gray back and wings, white face, and peach and gray on the top of the head and back of the neck. Both have thin beaks and spin frantically in shallow water while feeding. They prefer wetlands but will swim in deeper water.

COLOR: White, gray, and rust

HEAD: Small and round with a needle-thin bill

GISS: The shape and size of a spinning tennis ball, with a long, thin beak

RANGE: Western and central North America and along the Gulf Coast

FORSTER'S TERN *(For-sters turn)*

There may be over a dozen species of terns in North America. Terns look like delicate origami versions of gulls, with their pointed wings and thin, forked tails. Forster's terns are white with gray wings and a black cap. Forster's have thin orange beaks with a black tip. In winter, they have white faces with a black smudge near the eye. They live anywhere the water is calm, be it fresh water, brackish water, or salt water.

COLOR: White, gray, and black

HEAD: Flat with a long, pointed bill

GISS: Delicate, origami-like, the shape and size of a paper airplane

RANGE: Widespread in North America

AMERICAN OYSTERCATCHER
(Ah-mer-i-can oy-stir-cat-sher)

Dark brown on the back with white undersides, oystercatchers have black heads and necks and a long, thin orange beak. Their eyes are bright yellow, and if your binoculars are strong, you might detect an oddly shaped pupil or an extra fleck in the pupil. Recent studies suggest those are females. On the West Coast, you might spot an all-dark version called a black oystercatcher.

COLOR: Dark brown, white, and black

HEAD: Small and round, with a long, neon orange beak

GISS: The shape and size of a thick softball, with a long beak and long legs

RANGE: Coasts of North America

SNOW GOOSE *(sno goo-ss)*

Snow geese come in two different color morphs (the way they are hatched). One is white with black on the wingtips. Dark morph birds have a dark gray body with a white head and white under the tail. The birds gather by the millions during migration, creating quite the spectacle in New Mexico, Colorado, and Nebraska. They breed in the Arctic tundra.

COLOR: White, gray, and black

HEAD: Round, with a dainty, rounded beak

GISS: The shape and size of a football, with a long neck

RANGE: Central North America and parts of Alaska

RING-NECKED DUCK
(ree-ng neh-ked duh-k)

This poorly named duck has a very hard-to-see purple iridescent ring around its dark blue-black neck. Males have a dark head, black back, and tail with a light gray body and white ring around a gray bill with a black tip. Females have a black head, black back, and gray body. White feathers surround the beak, which is gray with a black tip. They can be found on ponds, lakes, and rivers.

COLOR: Black, gray, and purple

HEAD: Black, with a lump on the back of the head and yellow eye

GISS: The shape and size of a football, with a lumpy-looking head

RANGE: Throughout most of North and South America

MALE

FEMALE

BUFFLEHEAD *(buff-el-hed)*

These birds look like very tiny black-and-white ducks. Males are white with a black back. They have a greenish-purple and iridescent head with a bold white patch on the back. Females are dark gray with a noticeably white cheek patch. Northern flickers are crucial to their range because these birds nest in old flicker nest cavities. They breed in Alaska and Canada but can be found anywhere there is water in North America, when not breeding.

COLOR: Black, white, and dark gray

HEAD: Round with a dainty beak

GISS: The shape of a football but half the size

RANGE: Widespread in North America

MALE

FEMALE

RUDDY DUCK *(rud-eee duh-ck)*

Ruddy ducks are tiny and compact with stiff tails that they some-times hold straight up in the air. Males are rusty brown, with a black tail, black head, white cheek, and sky-blue bill. Females are mottled brown and gray, with a dark cap, black bill, and a darker gray back. Males resemble females in the winter but retain the white cheek patch.

COLOR: Rust, black, and gray

HEAD: Round and males have a large, rounded sky-blue bill and a white cheek patch

GISS: The shape of a football but half the size, with a stiff upright tail

RANGE: The US and central Canada

FEMALE

MALE

NORTHERN SHOVELER
(nor-thurn shove-ler)

The first thing you notice on this duck is the giant, shovel-like bill. Hence their name. Males have green heads, white-and-rusty bodies, sky-blue wing patches, and an enormous rounded black bill. Females are mottled buff and brown with an enormous black-and-orange bill. The females are unique in that when they are flushed off (startled into taking off) their nests, they will defecate on the eggs, presumably as a deterrent to a predator trying to eat them.

COLOR: Green, white, brown, and black

HEAD: Giant, shovel-like beak

GISS: The shape and size of a football, with a giant bill

RANGE: North America

FEMALE

MALE

AMERICAN WIGEON
(Ah-mer-i-can widg-un)

Some refer to this duck as the "bald pate" for the white forehead stripe on the male. Males are brown with a gray face, iridescent green stripe from the eye, and white stripe over the head. Females are reddish-brown with a gray face and gray bill. This vegetarian-ish duck gives a squeaky whistling call rather than a quack. They live near any water that is not ocean.

COLOR: Brown and gray

HEAD: Round head, dainty gray bill

GISS: The shape and size of a football

RANGE: Widespread in North America

FEMALE

MALE

A long and elegant duck, males are gray with a brown head and white chest, with a thin, pointy black tail. Females are gray with a thin tail and a dark beak. These birds forage in agricultural fields and then head to water. They eat seeds, snails, aquatic invertebrates, rice, corn, and anything else they can fit in their beaks. They tend to migrate at night.

COLOR: Gray, white, and brown

HEAD: Round, short gray bill

GISS: The shape of a football but slightly smaller in size

RANGE: North America

FEMALE

MALE

COMMON MERGANSER
(kom-on mer-gans-zer)

Males are white and sometimes pinkish with a dark green head and bright orange thin beak. Females are gray with a rusty crested head, orange beak, and white chin patch. These birds tend to be around deep lakes and rivers and will use tree cavities for nesting.

COLOR: White, green, brown, and pinkish

HEAD: Flat with a thin orange beak

GISS: The shape and size of a football but stretched out

RANGE: Northeastern and western North America

FEMALE

MALE

During the breeding season, adult common loons have a dark green head that looks black on cloudy days. Their backs are speckled with white, and they have dark wings and a white belly. In winter, they have gray heads and bodies with white chins and bellies. Common loon feet are so far back on their bodies that they cannot walk on land, but it helps them to swim underwater. They require large bodies of water in order to take off to fly.

COLOR: Black, white, gray, and green

HEAD: Oval with a fishing spear–like beak

GISS: The shape of a submarine and the size of a beach ball

RANGE: Large bodies of water in North America

WINTER

SUMMER

BLACK TERN *(blak turn)*

One of the smallest terns in the United States, black terns have a jet-black body; thin bill; long, pointy, dark gray wings; and white under the tail. In winter, the head, chest, and belly turn white with dark patches on the head and face. Black terns are found in freshwater marshes in loose colonies, meaning their nests are near one another but spaced several feet apart.

COLOR: Black, dark gray, and white

HEAD: Round, thin black beak

GISS: Delicate like origami, the shape and size of a paper airplane

RANGE: Widespread in the US

CASPIAN TERN *(Kas-pee-an turn)*

This robust tern is the largest of its species and one of the more common terns seen in migration. These white-and-gray birds sport the black cap common to most tern species but have a hefty, thick, bright orange beak. They have noticeably pointed wings in flight. They tend to nest in open habitats.

COLOR: White, gray, and black

HEAD: Flat head, thick orange beak

GISS: Robust, the shape and size of a sideways double-scoop ice-cream cone

RANGE: North America

AMERICAN BITTERN *(Ah-mer-i-can bit-hern)*

These birds are heard more than seen. In the spring, they sound like a sump pump. They are medium-sized herons with yellow-and-black beaks and striped brown-and-bluff plumage. These birds are basically shape changers: they can be round and shaggy or sleek. When threatened, they will extend their necks and point their beaks straight in the air to blend in with the long lines of the surrounding reeds and grasses.

COLOR: Brown and buff

HEAD: Flat with a spear-like beak

GISS: Shaggy and squat, the shape and size of a beach ball

RANGE: Wetlands of North America

WILSON'S SNIPE *(Will-sons sn-ie-p)*

This round bird is brown and striped with barring along the flanks and a comically long bill. Vertical barring on the head separates it from the similar-looking woodcock, which also has a long, tapered beak. This bird has a unique habit of perching on fence posts or the tops of trees to call. In the spring, these birds will fly for hours making a "woo woo woo woo" sound with their tail feathers.

COLOR: Brown

HEAD: Big eyed with a super-long, tapered beak

GISS: The shape and size of a softball, on sticks

RANGE: Widespread in North America

AMERICAN WOODCOCK
(Ah-mer-i-can wood-cok)

These birds are usually spotted when you nearly step on them and they explosively fly away. They camouflage well in low vegetation; in fact, they nest on the ground. Woodcocks are round, buff-colored-and-brown birds with black horizontal stripes on the head and vertical black stripes on the back. They boast a long, thin bill, and have a funky, bouncy gait. In spring at dusk, males make a kazoo-like "peent" sound and then do wild spins in the air while the females watch in judgment.

COLOR: Brown, buff, and black

HEAD: Big eyes, incredibly long, tapered beak

GISS: The shape and size of a tennis ball, on sticks

RANGE: The eastern US

AMERICAN DIPPER *(Ah-mer-i-can dip-her)*

Dippers are stout, round birds with a habit of bouncing or "dipping." They are dark gray with a brownish head and a thin black beak. The dipper often dives looking for aquatic invertebrates but will perch on one rock or log for long periods. If you're along a fast-moving stream and see a rock covered in bird poop, chances are good that a dipper will show up soon.

COLOR: Dark gray

HEAD: Round with a small, thin beak

GISS: Bouncy, the shape and size of a softball

RANGE: The western US and Canada, into Alaska

SIX RAPTORS

TURKEY VULTURE
(terr-key vul-chur)

This large, dark bird holds its wings in a V shape in flight, and rocks from side to side, like a child learning to ride a bike. Wings show gray all along the edges in flight. Turkey vultures sometimes soar along with much smaller black vultures, looking for food, like carrion and garbage, by smell.

COLOR: Black, gray, and red

HEAD: Bald, red head with a white beak

GISS: Similar to a bald eagle in appearance, chunky, the shape and size of a cinder block

RANGE: Widespread in the US and Canada

COOPER'S HAWK *(Koop-her's hauk)*

These thin hawks are blue on the back and orange on the belly and have a long tail and bright red eyes. Immatures are brown on the back with white-and-brown-streaked bellies and yellow eyes. In flight, Cooper's hawks have short wings, with a distinctly long tail. Females are much larger than males. They are very adept at dodging trees in a thick forest. Typically hawks of the thick forest, they have adapted well to urban areas.

COLOR: Blue and orange

FACE: Dark cap, maniacal red eye in adults

GISS: The shape and size of a bowling pin

RANGE: The US and Canada

RED-TAILED HAWK *(red-taled hauk)*

The most common hawk in North America, its color varies greatly. It is generally brown with white spots on the back, a dark belly band under a creamy-colored chest, and a rusty-red tail. Immatures can be lighter with a brown striped tail. And then some birds are dark chocolate brown or almost completely white. This is the hawk you are most likely to see perched on light posts on highways. They eat mammals like rabbits, squirrels, and mice and have adapted to eating pigeons in urban areas.

COLOR: Brown, creamy white, and rusty red

HEAD: Large, with a big, hooked beak

GISS: Chunky, the shape and size of a cinder block

RANGE: Widespread in the US and Canada

ADULT

JUVENILE

GREAT HORNED OWL *(grate hornd ow-ll)*

This large owl boasts two distinctive feather tufts on the top of its head and bright yellow eyes. Generally mottled brown, white, and gray, some birds can be a very light, almost-cream color, and others can be a dark gray. This is the owl that makes the stereo-typical hooting sound. They live in numerous habitats and eat just about anything they can get their talons into, from large mammals like skunks to birds like blue jays.

COLOR: Brown, gray, and white

HEAD: Big, with two large tufts, yellow eyes, and a hooked beak

GISS: The shape and size of a cinder block, with two tufts

RANGE: Widespread in the US and Canada

DID YOU KNOW . . .

Young great horned owls make a loud high-pitched screeching sound that some people mistake for a fox. The tufts on the owl's head serve more as a communi-cation and camouflage device than a tool for listening. Like those of most owls, the ears of a great horned owl are slits on both sides of its face. They are uneven, which allows the owl to pinpoint prey by sound while hunting. Their disc-shaped face allows them to capture sound, and the small stiff feathers guide the sounds to the owls' ears. If you see an owl bobbing its head back and forth, that is its way of trying to triangulate exactly where a sound is coming from.

BALD EAGLE *(balld EE-gull)*

This large raptor soars with its wings held flat. Adults are iconic with their brown bodies and white heads and tails. Immature birds are highly variable in color, from all black to black and mottled white. Bald eagles are frequently found around fish kills, garbage dumps, roadkill, and farms. They prefer wooded areas with tall, mature trees next to large bodies of water. The founders of the US thought that the bald eagle made a good national symbol of authority, and that symbol still stands today.

COLOR: Brown, white, and black

HEAD: Round and bald, with a big bill

GISS: Chunky, the shape and size of a cinder block

RANGE: Widespread in the US and Canada

ADULT

JUVENILE

OSPREY *(oss-pray)*

Osprey only eat fish, so are found near large bodies of water like rivers and oceans. They are large brown-and-white birds, shaggy-looking on the backs of their heads. They make these huge stick nests on just about anything with a 360° view, including lights over a football field.

COLOR: Brown and white

HEAD: Shaggy back of head, with a yellow eye and a large, hooked beak

GISS: Large, the size of a beach ball, shaggy raptor

RANGE: The US and Canada

AMERICAN KESTREL *(Ah-mer-i-can kess-trell)*

These dainty little falcons can be found in cities perched on church steeples or power lines or watching for grasshoppers and rodents along farm fields. Males are orange with blue wings, a rusty tail, and black spots. Females are rusty orange with black spots all over with blue on the head. These birds typically bob their tails when they land and often hover in flight over warm mouse urine, which they can spot in the UV spectrum. After all, where there is urine, there is usually a mouse.

COLOR: Blue and orange, with black spots

HEAD: Round with a short, hooked beak

GISS: The shape and size of a double-scoop ice-cream cone

RANGE: The US and Canada

MERLIN *(murr-lihn)*

This small falcon flies quickly, as if it's late for a meeting. Males are blue-gray on the back, with brown-and-white-streaked chests, and long tails with a dark band on the tip. Females are brownish-gray on the back with brown and buff on the chest. Birds can be dark to very light depending on their geographic location. They are incredibly vocal around their nests and make a rapid staccato screech all day. This adaptable falcon can be found in a variety of habitats, from boreal forests to metropolitan areas, usually near some form of water.

COLOR: Gray, blue, brown, and white

HEAD: Round with a dainty, hooked beak

GISS: The shape and size of a double-scoop ice-cream cone

RANGE: The US and Canada

MALE

FEMALE

BARRED OWL *(bard ow-ll)*

Barred owls tend to sound more like monkeys than owls when hooting. They are light colored with brown streaking, no tufts, and brown eyes. They have an incredibly varied diet that includes birds, rodents, crawfish, caterpillars, snakes, and mussels. They live in the woods, especially near water like a floodplain forest or wooded swamp, and can be active during the day.

COLOR: Cream and brown

HEAD: Round with brown eyes

GISS: The shape and size of a baskeball

RANGE: The eastern US and Canada

BROAD-WINGED HAWK *(braaud-winged hauk)*

This smallish hawk has a dark brown head and back and a bold black-and-white tail with thicker bands than those of the red-shouldered hawk. Immature broad-wings have a brown striped tail. These birds are noisy around their nests, making a high-pitched two-note whistle. In autumn, they gather in flocks of thousands called "kettles" as they head south.

COLOR: Brown, white, and black

HEAD: Round with a small, hooked beak

GISS: The shape and size of a bowling pin but dainty

RANGE: The eastern US and southern Canada

SCREECH OWL *(skreech ow-ll)*

These small owls with feather tufts on either side of their head can be mottled gray or rusty red (eastern) or only gray (western). Their call is more of a tremulous horse whinny than an actual screech, and can be heard in suburban neighborhoods or deep in the woods. They eat a variety of foods, including large insects, small rodents, small birds, and reptiles. They are found anywhere with trees that have cavities large enough for them.

COLOR: Gray and rust

HEAD: Angry yellow eyes with feather tufts

GISS: The shape and size of a softball

RANGE: Widespread in the US

DID YOU KNOW . . .

Either male or female eastern screech owl can be red or gray. During mating season you may find two grays nesting together or a red and a gray nesting together. Screech owls will readily use large human-made birdhouses for nesting or sleeping during the day. They often perch right at the opening of a wood duck box they have claimed. Many owls will get "mobbed" by songbirds during the day. Because screech owls are small, it's usually the tiny songbirds that yell at them. An angry sounding chickadee or robin will often alert people to the presence of a screech owl trying to sleep during the day.

RAPTORS

RED-SHOULDERED HAWK
(red-shole-durd hauk)

This very chatty hawk calls all year-round. Overall brown with noticeable rusty-red shoulders, a rusty chest, and black-and-white wings with distinctive "windows," these birds can vary from darker to lighter. Immatures have a brown-and-buff tail. Known to steal food off grills, they typically eat other birds, amphibians, reptiles, and small mammals.

COLOR: Brown, rust, black, and white

HEAD: Shaggy with a hooked beak

GISS: The shape and size of a bowling pin

RANGE: The eastern US and the West Coast

SWAINSON'S HAWK *(Swane-sunz hauk)*

This is a thin hawk of the grasslands. Adults are generally dark gray on the back, with a reddish bib, a white chest, and white outlining the hooked beak. But some birds are completely dark brown. Their

wings are long and somewhat pointed in flight. They eat mammals and reptiles but will follow farmers plowing fields or harvesting to catch grasshoppers and other insects in flight.

COLOR: Gray, white, and rusty brown

HEAD: Flat with a hooked beak

GISS: The shape and size of a cinder block but lankier

RANGE: The eastern US and Canada

BURROWING OWL *(burr-ow-ing ow-ll)*

The burrowing owl has a tiny owl body on long legs and has a mixture of brown-and-white feathers, with a distinct white unibrow and chin. Sometimes, you will only spot their heads as they stick out of old rodent holes. They eat lots of flying insects, and they live in open habitats, like grasslands and deserts, in burrows in the ground that they make or that prairie dogs or tortoises made.

COLOR: Brown and white

HEAD: Bright yellow eyes set in a round head with a unibrow

GISS: The shape and size of a football, with stick legs

RANGE: The western United States and Florida

MISSISSIPPI KITE
(Miss-siz-ippi ky-te)

Sleek and silvery gray, adults have a light-colored head with a dark red eye, dark gray back and belly, pointed black wings that show patches of white in flight, and a flared tail. These birds hunt in open areas but will nest in woods and windbreaks on farms. They eat large insects, reptiles, amphibians, mammals, and birds. This is the most common of the five kite species in North America.

COLOR: Gray, black, and white

HEAD: Round, with a red eye and a hooked beak

GISS: The shape and size of a bowling pin

RANGE: The southern and western US

RAPTORS

PEREGRINE FALCON
(pear-a-green fal-kon)

Adult peregrines are dark blue on the back with a dark hood and distinctive vertical stripe going down under the eye. Their chests can be cream to rusty with horizontal striping. Falcons have obvious pointed wings in flight. They nest around high cliffs or skyscrapers and hunt open areas, especially near water. They mostly eat other birds, like pigeons and flickers.

COLOR: Dark blue, cream, and brown

HEAD: Striped under the eye with a hooked beak

GISS: Erect, slim, the shape and size of a bowling pin

RANGE: Widespread in North America

DID YOU KNOW . . .

Peregrines are fierce defenders of their territory and will chase out much larger birds of prey like red-tailed hawks and even bald eagles. Their speed makes them a formidable foe. Most birds of prey are fast when diving for prey in the sky, but peregrines have been clocked going over 200 miles an hour in a dive. Their stiff wing feathers make them faster than hawks, but the feathers are vulnerable to breaking if the falcon is diving for something on the ground. Most peregrines catch their prey in flight, unlike other hawks.

PRAIRIE FALCON *(prayer-ee fal-kon)*

Light brown on back with a white chest and brown spots, this falcon, like all others, has a distinct, dark vertical stripe under each eye. In flight, it has noticeably pointed wings with dark undersides. They hunt wide-open spaces in the western part of the country.

COLOR: Light brown, white, and black

HEAD: Round with a vertical stripe and hooked beak

GISS: The shape and size of a bowling pin

RANGE: The western US

ROUGH-LEGGED HAWK *(ruff-leg-d hauk)*

Their color can vary a lot, but these birds typically have a frosty-white head with a dark eyeline, dark back and wings, and a thick, dark belly band and striped tail. Yet some birds are almost completely black. These hawks tend to hold their wings in a V shape in flight and to hover. They breed in the Arctic and nest on cliffs or open tundra.

COLOR: Black, white, and gray

HEAD: Round and shaggy, with an eyeline and a dainty beak

GISS: Shaggy, the shape and of a cinder block but a bit smaller

RANGE: The US and Canada

Index

Acknowledgments

I'd like to thank anyone who has ever shared a bird story with me; I file them away. I'd also like to thank Brian Goodspeed, Kara Snow, Michelle Kalantari, Gayle Deutsch, Joey Sundvall, Curt Rawn, Dan Dressler, Nikki Koval, Dr. and Mrs. Paul Strange, Frank Taylor, Mark Martell, and everyone who helps to make eBird work.

About the Author

Sharon Stiteler was given a Peterson Field Guide when she was seven years old and snapped. She loves birds; it's just the way she's wired. She's written several books and articles on birds. Her writing has appeared in *Audubon* magazine, the *Washington Post*, and *Outdoor News*. She appears regularly on TV and radio programs answering bird questions. When not leading bird tours or speaking at birding and nature events, she works for the National Park Service.

CPSIA information can be obtained
at www.ICGtesting.com
Printed in the USA
LVHW071511290522
720010LV00002B/3

9 781638 783480